OutdoorLife
THE SPORTSMAN'S AUTHORITY SINCE 1898

If Nature Calls... Hang Up!

A Classic Collection of Outdoor Humor

P9-EAO-096

CREATIVE
PUBLISHING
international

MINNETONKA, MINNESOTA

Creative Publishing international, Inc.
5900 Green Oak Drive
Minnetonka, MN 55343
1-800-328-3895

Chairman: Iain Macfarlane
President/CEO: David D. Murphy
Vice President/Retail Sales & Marketing: James Knapp
Creative Director: Lisa Rosenthal

IF NATURE CALLS . . . HANG UP!
Executive Editor, Outdoor Group: Don Oster
Managing Editor: Jill Anderson
Associate Creative Director: Brad Springer
Photo Researcher: Angie Hartwell
Mac Designers: Joe Fahey, Laurie Kristensen, Brad Webster
Copy Editors: Janice Cauley, Lee Engfer, Hazel Jensen
Photographers: Tate Carlson, Andrea Rugg
Production Services Manager: Kim Gerber

Printed on American paper by: R. R. Donnelley & Sons Co.

10   9   8   7   6   5   4   3   2   1

Library of Congress Cataloging-in-Publication Data

If nature calls-- hang up! : a collection of outdoor humor.
     p.   cm.
   At head of title: Outdoor life.
   ISBN 0-86573-106-3 (soft cover)
    1. Hunting Anecdotes.   2. Fishing Anecdotes.   3. Hunting Humor.
4. Fishing Humor.   I. Creative Publishing International.
II. Outdoor life (Denver, Colo.) III. Title: Outdoor life.
SK33.I3   1999
799.2'02'07--dc21   99-38860

table of contents

iNtRoductioN

"Next time tHe gReat outdooRs caLLiNg,
you'd BetteR HaNg up!"

$\mathcal{I}$n one form or another, good clean outdoor-related humor has always been a part of *Outdoor Life* magazine's product. From the mid-1900s to the present, rich humor has been presented in feature stories sprinkled through various issues. Other elements appearing in the 1950s and 1960s were cartoons, short yarns called "Tall But Short" and a long-running series of short quips submitted by readers called "The Gist of It." In the early 1980s the humor torch was passed to Patrick F. McManus, who writes an every-issue rib-tickler that continues today.

In *If Nature Calls . . . Hang Up!* we have lifted the best of the features, McManus, cartoons, "Tall But Shorts" and "Gists," compiling them into an extremely funny anthology commemorating 50 years of *Outdoor Life* humor. You'll laugh yourself silly at features like "Lightning-Rod Dog," "I'm Sick of Moose," "Terror of the Pack Train," "Sucker Bait," "Poof—No Eyebrows!" and more than two dozen others. So sit back, relax and have a good clean laugh at no one's expense.

Poof! No Eyebrows!

by Patrick F. McManus

Building a muzzleloader from scratch is risky business, especially when you work your way up to a sewer-pipe cannon too soon.

*J*UST AS I WAS ASSEMBLING THE ingredients for a small snack in the kitchen, the doorbell rang. My wife, Bun, went to answer it, and I heard her invite in Milt Slapshot, a neighbor who often seeks out my advice on matters pertaining to the sporting life.

"Is Pat home?" I heard Milt ask. "A fella told me he knows something about muzzleloading."

Realizing Bun could never resist a straight line like that, I jumped up and headed for the living room in the hope of stifling her.

"Does he ever!" she said, chortling. "Why, this very minute he's out in the kitchen loading his muzzle!"

A wife who chortles is an irritation, but one who also regards herself as a wit is a social nuisance. I grabbed Milt by the arm and guided him toward the den before Bun could embarrass the poor fellow further with another attempt at emulating Erma Bombeck.

"Stop the cackling, Milt," I told him. "It only encourages her."

Once his tasteless display of mirth had subsided, Milt explained that he was building a muzzleloader and needed some technical advice from me. A mutual acquaintance, one Retch Sweeney, had told him that I had once conducted extensive scientific research on primitive firearms. That was true. In fact, it would be difficult to find firearms more primitive than those utilized in my research.

"You've come to the right man," I said. "Yes, indeed. Now the first thing I need to know is, are you building it from a kit or from scratch?"

"A kit," Milt said.

"Good," I said. "Building muzzleloaders from scratch is a risky business, particularly when you work your way up to sewer pipe too soon. Now the first thing . . . "

"Sewer pipe?" Milt asked. "What do you mean, sewer pipe? Are you sure you know something about blackpowder?"

"Ha!" I replied. "Do you see my eyebrows?"

"No."

"Well, that should answer your question. All us experts on black-powder have bald eyes."

Actually, I do have eyebrows, but they are pale, sickly fellows, never having recovered from the shock of instant immolation 30 years ago. Having my eyebrows catch fire ranks as one of the more interesting experiences of my life, although I must say I didn't enjoy it much at the time.

Indeed, my somewhat faulty eyesight may be a direct result of having my eyebrows go up in smoke. Either it was that or the splash of Orange Crush soda pop with which my sidekick Retch Sweeney, ever quick to compound a catastrophe, doused the flames.

As I explained to Milt, who had settled into a chair in the den and was attempting with some success to conceal his fascination, most of my early research into the mysteries of blackpowder took place during the year I was 14. Some of those experiments produced spectacular results, particularly the last one, which enabled Retch and me to attend the annual Halloween party as twin cinders.

The first experiment, in which my eyebrows were sacrificed to the cause of science, consisted of placing a small pile of blackpowder on a bicycle seat and touching a lighted match to it. I can no longer recall why a bicycle seat was employed as part of the apparatus, but I am sure my co-researcher and I had sound reasons for it at the time. In any case, we proved conclusively that a match flame serves as an excellent catalyst on gunpowder. I later concluded that the experiment might have been improved upon in only two ways: to have placed the powder on *Retch's* bicycle seat and to have let *him* hold the match. Instead, he chose to stand in awe of the experiment and about 10 feet away, sucking absently on a bottle of Orange Crush. On the other hand, my sacrifice was not without its reward, since bald eyes and a hole burnt in my bicycle seat made great conversation openers with girls at school.

The success of the experiment had to be withheld from the rest of the scientific community for fear our parents would find out about it. Unfortunately, my mother inadvertently discovered the secret.

"Is anything the matter?" Mom asked during supper the evening after the bicycle-seat experiment.

"No," I replied, casually. "Why do you ask?"

"Oh, nothing in particular," she said. "It just seems a little odd, your wearing sunglasses and a cap at the dinner table."

She then expressed her desire that I remove both glasses and cap instantly, sooner if possible. After some debate over the finer points of dinner table propriety, I complied.

As expected, Mom responded with the classic question favored by the parents of young blackpowder experimenters everywhere: "WHAT HAPPENED TO YOUR EYEBROWS?"

Looking surprised and fingering the scorched area above my eyes, I tried to convey the impression it was news to me that my eyebrows were missing, as if they might have dropped off unnoticed or been mislaid at school. It takes a better actor than I, however, to pull off a convincing performance to the effect that one's eyebrows can disappear by some means undetected by their owner.

The truth was soon extracted from me with an efficiency that would have been the envy of medieval counterintelligence agents. This was followed by a bit of parental advice. But scarcely had this parental advice ceased reverberating among the rafters than I was already plotting my next experiments for unlocking the mysteries of blackpowder.

The discovery by Retch and me that we could purchase blackpowder in bulk from a local dealer was to have great impact on our lives, not to mention various parts of our anatomies. The dealer in question was the proprietor of Grogan's War Surplus, Hardware & Gun Emporium, none other than that old reprobate, Henry P. Grogan himself. We weren't at all sure Grogan would sell a couple of scruffy, goof-off kids something as potentially dangerous as blackpowder. Our first attempt at making a purchase was, therefore, cloaked in subtlety and subterfuge.

"Howdy, Mr. Grogan," we opened with, both of us so casual we were fit to burst.

"Howdy, boys. What can I do for you—assuming, of course, you got cash in your pockets and ain't just here to finger the merchandise?"

"Oh, we got cash," I said. "Uh, Retch, why don't you read Mr. Grogan our list?"

"Uh, OK, heh, heh. Yeah, well, here goes—one GI mess kit, one helmet liner, a parachute harness, a pound of blackpowder, and let's see, now, do you have any of those neat camouflage jackets left?"

To our chagrin, a look of concern came into Grogan's eyes. "Gosh, boys, I don't know if I should . . . It just don't seem right to sell you two young fellows . . . Oh, what the heck! Elmer Peabody wanted me to save those last two camouflage jackets for him, but I'll let you have 'em. Now, how much gun powder was that you wanted—a pound?"

In all fairness to Grogan, I must admit that he did warn us that severe bodily harm could result from improper use of the blackpowder. His exact words, if I remember correctly, were, "You boys set off any of that stuff near my store and I'll peel your hides!"

Since getting your hide peeled tends to smart a good deal, we abided by Henry P.'s warning.

The blackpowder we bought from Grogan had been compressed by the manufacturer into shiny black pellets, a form intended, I believe, to make it less volatile. Even before mashing them into powder, we found it was possible to touch off the pellets if they were first piled on a bicycle seat and a match held to them. The pellets did not ignite immediately even then, apparently for the purpose of tricking the person holding the match into taking a closer look at what was occurring on the bicycle seat. Then—POOF!—no eyebrows.

Our first muzzleloaders were small and crude, but, as our technological skill and knowledge increased, they gradually became large and crude. We never did develop a satisfactory triggering mechanism. On the average shot, you could eat a sandwich between the time the trigger was pulled and the gun discharged. A typical muzzleloader test would go something like this:

RETCH: OK, I'm going to squeeze the trigger now. There!

MUZZLELOADER: *Snick! Pop! Ssssss . . .*

ME: Good. It looks like it's working. Better start aiming at the tin can.

MUZZLELOADER: *Ssss . . . fizt . . . ssss . . .*

RETCH: Say, give me a bit of that sandwich, will you?

ME: Sure.

MUZZLELOADER: *. . . sss . . . sput . . . ss . . . putt . . . ss . . .*

RETCH: What time is it?

ME: About time for me to —

MUZZLELOADER: … *sssst* — *POOT!*

RETCH (enveloped in cloud of smoke): How was my aim?

ME: I think it was pretty good, but the muzzle velocity leaves something to be desired. As soon as the smoke clears, reach over and pick up the ball and we'll load her up again.

Even as we increased the range of our muzzleloaders, the delay in the firing mechanism discouraged us from using them on game. If we had used one of them for rabbit hunting, say, we would have had to squeeze the trigger and then hope a rabbit would happen to be running by when the gun discharged. Squeezing the trigger before your game appears over the far horizon is the ultimate in leading a moving target.

Since we had up to three minutes of lead time on stationary targets, hunting with our muzzleloaders seemed somewhat impractical. There was also the probable embarrassment of having our shots bounce off the game. It didn't seem worth the risk. A hunter can stand only so much humiliation.

Our first muzzleloader was a small-caliber Deringer, the ammunition for which consisted mostly of dried peas. This prompted Retch to remark derisively to a tin-can target, "All right, Ringo, drop your iron or I'll fill you full of dried peas."

"OK, OK," I said, "I get your drift. We'll move up to the hard stuff—marbles, ball bearings and golf balls."

It was a mistake, though, and I knew it. Once you start escalating, there's no stopping until you achieve the ultimate weapon. Within a couple of months, we were turning out muzzleloaders in the .80-caliber range. Then we got into the large-caliber stuff. Finally, we decided the time had come to stop monkeying around with black-powder pistols and rifles. We'd had some close calls. We had reached the point where there was some doubt in our minds whether we might be firing a muzzleloader or touching off a bomb. Thus it was with considerable relief that we abandoned our clandestine manufacture and testing of pistols and rifles. After all, a cannon would be much safer; you didn't have to hold it.

The cannon was constructed of sewer pipe, 2x4s, baby-carriage wheels, rubber inner-tube bands, a clothespin, baling wire and various other odds and ends, all of which, blending into a single, symmetrical unity, neared perfection on the scale of beauty. A croquet ball was commandeered from the Sweeney backyard for use as shot. In our enthusiasm of the moment, it was thought the croquet ball could be returned to the set after it was recovered from the firing range. Alas, it was not to be so.

Attired in our muskrat-skin hats, which we had sewn up ourselves, we mounted our bicycles and, with cannon in tow, set off for the local golf course, where a fairway would serve as a firing range, a putting green as a target.

As we had hoped, the golf course turned out to be deserted. We quickly wheeled the cannon into firing position and began the loading procedure.

"Think that's enough powder?" Retch asked.

"Better dump in some more," I advised. "That croquet ball is pretty heavy."

"And there's some for good measure," Retch said.

The croquet ball fit a little too tightly, but we managed to ram it down the barrel.

Then we both took up positions alongside the cannon to witness the rare and wonderful spectacle of a sewer pipe firing a croquet ball down a golf-course fairway.

"Ready, aim, fire!" I commanded.

Retch tripped the firing mechanism.

Eventually, the thunder was replaced by clanging bells inside our heads, the shattered pieces of earth and sky fell back into place, and the wobbly world righted itself. Retch and I limped over to the shade of a utility shed and sat down to relax a bit and collect our senses. Presently, a deputy sheriff drove up. He stood for a moment gazing at the haze of smoke wafting gently over the golf course, the patch of smoldering turf ringed by fragments of sewer pipe, baby carriage wheels and pieces of 2x4. Then, hoisting up his gun belt, he sauntered over to us.

"You boys know anything about an explosion out this way?" he asked.

"What kind of explosion?" Retch asked.

"A *big* explosion."

I was still so stunned I couldn't even think up a good lie. Anyway, I knew the deputy had us cold.

"Now, what I want to know," the deputy went on, "is why are you two boys sitting out here behind this shed smoking?"

"Shucks," I said, "if you'd been out here a little earlier, you'd have seen us while we were still on fire!"

I thought for sure he was going to haul us off to jail, but instead he just smiled, took one last look at the smouldering debris, and started to saunter back to his car. "Well, if you fellas turn up any information about the explosion," he said over his shoulder, "I'd appreciate it if you'd let me know. I don't reckon there'll be another one, do you?"

"Nope," Retch and I said in unison.

Then the deputy stopped and kicked gingerly at something on the ground in front of him. It was Retch's muskrat hat! The deputy turned and gave us a sympathetic look. "Too bad about your dog," he said.

The cannon pretty well quelled our enthusiasm for building our own muzzleloaders from scratch. Not only had it made a big impression on us, it had made numerous small impressions. Years later, while I was undergoing a physical examination, the doctor commented on some bumps under my skin.

"Pay them no mind, Doc," I told him. "They're just pieces of sewer pipe."

At this juncture of my recitation, Milt Slapshot jumped up and headed for the door.

"Thanks," he said. "You've answered my question."

"Gee," I said. "I've even forgotton what the question was. But if you need any help putting your muzzleloader kit together, Milt, just give me a call."

He hasn't called yet. I suppose he's been tied up at the office a lot lately.

taLL
But
SHORt

Us duck hunters were discussing duck decoys, and naturally each one thought his own favorite stool was the only one worth a hoot. Freddie, an old-timer, took the gab as long as he could. "Decoys!" he sneered. "What do we know about decoys anymore? Back in the old days, when a man could use a tame duck for a stool, he got some shooting. And my pop had the best live decoy of 'em all."

"Sho nuff, Freddie?" I said. "Tell us about it."

"Well sir, pop had a trained mallard hen. Every time he came out the back door with his old double-gun over his shoulder, why, that duck would just naturally fall in behind him.

"When they'd reach pop's favorite pond, that there old duck would hop in and swim around, hollering her head off. After she persuaded some wildfowl to land on the pond, she'd dive under the surface and hold onto the grass on the bottom till she heard both barrels of pop's gun go off.

"They had good times, pop and the duck, and he grew real fond of her. When he lost her he just quit gunning, and never went out again."

"How did he lose her?" I asked.

"Well, one day he dropped his double-gun and busted the stock. He wanted to go out duck hunting that day, so he borrowed a gun from a friend. Then him and the mallard went out. And just like usual she attracted a flock of ducks down onto the water. Then she dove and hung onto the bottom grass. And by golly, she never come up."

"What happened?"

"Well, it was this way. When pop started out, he forgot to tell the duck that the gun he borrowed had only a single barrel. She drownded waiting for the second shot."

W. L. Moore Jr.

Eli Sly and the Decoy Deer

by Norman Strung

WHEN eLi sLy saw an oLd stuffed deer Head for saLe, an idea was BORN. WHat foLLowed was tHe fuNNiest HUNtiNG season ever ON His moNtaNa RaNCH.

"**Y**ONKERS"—THAT'S WHAT Eli Sly calls most hunters who visit his Montana ranch. The term has its origin in two hunters he once guided. They were from Yonkers, New York, and were so green that they let deer after deer slip by them. The pair seemed incapable of hitting anything beyond 50 yards.

Last season was a particularly frustrating one for Eli. Big deer were in short supply on his ranch, and a dry, warm fall made even dumb forkhorns unapproachable. By midseason, although some 20 hunters had passed through his gateposts and covered the pastures and coulees on the ranch that sprawled over two counties, only three tags had been filled.

True, there had been opportunities, but few hunters had connected. Reasons had been cited—spooked deer, running deer, out-of-range deer; but at the root of all the muffs and misses lay the inescapable fact that most of those hunters had been, well . . . Yonkers.

Then one day at a farm auction, Eli's date with destiny was heaved upon the block, and he recognized it immediately. It was a mounted mule deer head, obviously some snowbound rancher's attempt at taxidermy. It was moth-eaten and dusty and had an ear split that revealed the tin bolster inside, and a nose painted brown instead of black. But it had a giant rack. The tobacco-chewing, clod-kicking ranchers and farmers in attendance had a laugh when Eli's bid of a dollar bought the mount.

"What in blazes are you gonna do with that thing?" one of them asked.

Eli just chuckled.

a hunt with Eli always begins as dawn warms and glows on the horizon. His ranch road runs east from the corrals and up a dry coulee; then it forks to the south and north, two miles away. Eli always takes the south fork and drives a route that scribes a huge circle past wheat fields, twisting canyons, sparse stands of juniper and ponderosa pine, sandstone ledges, washouts and sagebrush.

At selected points along this route, canyons are glassed, drives are organized, water holes are watched and hunters are counseled in the ways of mule deer.

There is a place not 100 yards before you get to the fork where a lone juniper has taken root at the base of a steep cut bank 25 yards from the side of the road. That was the spot Eli chose for the decoy deer.

It was perfect in many ways. Not only was it a little island of cover and shade where a deer would naturally hole up, but it was eminently visible too. You could glass it from the edge of the wheat field half a mile away, and the eight-foot cut bank made an ideal backstop for bullets.

In his cluttered shop Eli unearthed a five-foot piece of threaded steel pipe. He screwed a T on one end, then extended the T six inches on each side with more pipe. With plumber's tape he affixed the T to the wooden plaque in the back of the mounted head and put the contraption in the bed of his pickup, along with a 30-gallon oil drum and a rawhide. After a short ride and a little rigging, he'd be ready for any and all Yonkers.

He rolled the drum to the base of the cut bank and pushed the pipe supporting the mounted head into the soft earth at one end. Then he draped the hide over the drum. From as close as 25 yards away it looked very much like a breathing animal, and one helluva trophy to boot. Eli chuckled once again.

His object was not so much to play a practical joke as to prove a point. Many times he had whispered, "There's a deer," only to have the hunter at his side say, "Where? I don't see any deer," as the animal loped over a hill and out of sight. With that in mind, Eli coached every hunting party the same way. As he and his hunters neared the last stretch of wheat field a few miles before the fork in the road, Eli would mention that a great, gray ghost of a granddaddy buck had been seen near the ranch the day before. Hunters had caught no more than a glimpse of him, and no one had shot, so he was quite sure the animal was still around. "Keep a sharp eye out, now," Eli would warn. "The hunt's not over yet."

The first place he'd stop would be half a mile from the barrel buck, which was in plain view. He would suggest that somebody glass the coulee bottom below. The second stop was 125 yards from the deer. The road made a slight curve behind a hill that momentarily obscured the deer, and at that point, the decoy again popped into plain view.

"See anything down there?" Eli would ask.

The last place he'd stop was 25 yards from the phony deer. Many of the hunters still didn't see it!

Predictably, however, once the bogus buck was recognized, the hunters went crazy, and Eli was happy to encourage it. His first experiment took place with a young married couple whom we shall call Jack and Jill to preserve their anonymity. Though both were experienced hunters, they passed the deer twice without seeing it. On the third morning, Eli became more direct.

Stopping 70 yards from the cut bank, he said, "Jack, I think I see something up there. Get your binoculars."

No sooner had Jack put the glasses to his brows when he sucked in a sharp breath.

"Man alive! He's big!" he bellowed.

Eli cleared the driver's seat and yelled, "Take a good rest! Take a good rest!"

Jack rolled out one side and Jill tried to exit on the other, but her way was blocked by her rifle, which was wedged across the pickup's door. She kept throwing her weight against the stock, trying to make the rifle bend in the middle.

Meanwhile, Jack had assumed a kneeling position in the dirt. But instead of chambering a shell, he inexplicably hit his clip release, and his clip and shells fell into the grass. He tried to put the clip in backward.

"Man alive, he's big," he said again, his glazed eyes fixed upon the animal. The clip slipped from his grasp once more, and this time when he tried to push it back in it finally snapped home. Jack chambered a shell, shouldered the gun and fired.

Boom-kerwang! The muzzle blast was followed instantly by the almost melodious ring of vibrating metal.

"You missed," Eli yelled. "Shoot him again!"

Boom-kerwing! The note jumped an octave higher as the bullet struck a stiffer section of steel.

"I must have hit him then," Jack said.

"Well, his head is still up . . . shoot him between the eyes!"

By this time Jill had gathered herself together. She took aim from an offhand position and drilled the mounted head square in the middle of the skull. Sawdust shot out both ears like cartoon smoke from a character who had eaten a too-hot tamale.

There was puzzled silence for an eternal second. Jack turned, confused, to Eli, whose face was flushed from the strain of suppressed laughter. Tears were streaming down his cheeks. Realization crept across Jack's face.

"Sonofagun," he said. He grinned, looked down and kicked the dirt.

The statistics Eli amassed during that last half of hunting season were astounding. Out of 40 hunters he guided, not one saw the deer from half a mile away. At 125 yards, the sun played a major role in sightings. When the deer was in direct sunlight, nobody missed it. When the weather was cloudy, only about a third of the hunters saw it. And when the low afternoon sun cast a shadow from the lone juniper over the buck, no one saw it, even from 25 yards away!

There were other memorable incidents. Two hunters pumped 21 rounds into the pinging steel drum before they suspected that something wasn't quite right. Eli's hired man, after driving past the deer at least seven times, finally saw it at close range. He was on a piece of farm machinery without a gun, so he tried to sneak up on the animal with a tire iron, thinking it was wounded. The deer lost an ear in the ensuing battle. And two persons passed Eli's test with flying colors. One client refused to shoot because the animal had been spotted from a vehicle, and it offended his sense of fair chase. A neighbor of Eli's spotted the deer at the 125-yard post, stepped from the truck, shouldered his gun and after a long pause said, "You ain't gonna sucker me into shooting no stuffed deer."

To a man (and woman), they all took Eli's lesson good-naturedly, and a bit reflectively too, for it raised a nagging question: Just how many real deer does one overlook in the course of a season?

One question remains: How did I fare? Well, I never took the test. I happened to arrive at the ranch on a bright, sunny day when Eli wasn't guiding. He had sent some local hunters of his acquaintance into the north wheat field that morning, and they were due back any moment, so he told me about his experiment, and we laughed.

Just as we were about to go into the house, the muffled popping of gunfire rolled in from the east. *Boom . . . bang . . . kerwang, ping, ker-pow.*

Laugh wrinkles creased Eli's cheeks, and his eyes danced. "Sure got them Yonkers this year," he said, and he chuckled once more.

❖ ❖ ❖ ❖ ❖ ❖ ❖ ❖ ❖ ❖ ❖ ❖ ❖ ❖ ❖

Reᦞ aLeRt - Friends of a duck hunter who had a bad habit of shooting before the legal hour cured him by substituting for his ammo red flare 12 gauge shells used by the army as distress signals. The spectacular results above his blind changed his ways.
- Bud Boyd, SAN FRANCISCO (CA) CHRONICLE.

Quickie - Walter La Cross says his brother saw a muskie pick a frog off a sandbar in Conneaut Creek. Spotting the frog in the middle of a sandbar about six feet wide, the muskie swam upstream a bit, turned and came down full speed with the current, shot across the bar on his belly and gobbled up the frog en route. - Red Giesler, ERIE (PA) DISPATCH-HERALD.

❖ ❖ ❖ ❖ ❖ ❖ ❖ ❖ ❖ ❖ ❖ ❖ ❖ ❖ ❖

taLL
BuT
SHORT

We were setting around the campfire and we got to talking about mirages and how they could fool a fellow sure, even if he was an old-timer on the plains. One old puncher recollected a hand who was moving a herd of cattle through Montana in country he wasn't familiar with and he came on this wonderful rangeland with plenty of water and grazing, so he set his longhorns out there for the winter. It wasn't until he got back to the ranch in the spring with his cows and told the boss about it that he found out what he'd done. "Why, you fool," said the boss, "there ain't no good grazing in there. That was just a mirage."

"OK," said the hand, "but don't tell the cows, cause they're fat as butter."

Then another fellow told about how he was out hunting in Wyoming once and he saw a big mirage up ahead—a fine grove of trees. He knew it was a mirage, though, because it appeared all of a sudden. So he paid no attention to it.

"I just went on hunting," he said, "and pret' soon I run into a big grizzly bear. I give him a shot from my .45/70 but it didn't hurt him—just riled him up. He lets out a beller and starts for me, and I starts for elsewhere.

"Trouble was, there was no place to run, so I headed for the mirage. It looked comforting, anyway. The bear kept gaining and I kept running. Soon I was plump into the mirage forest, and when the bear gave a swipe at the seat of my pants, why, I just kinda made a leap up into one of the trees. Didn't do no good. I just fell flat on my face on the ground."

"Wow!" said one of the fellows. "What happened then?"

"Why, nothin'. Turned out that the bear was a mirage, too."

Jerry A. Ross

"giving him a tub bath got to be a nuisance."

"that harold's a card. that's him trying to make like an elk."

Terror of the Pack Train

by Dolores Brown

aLL OUR HORSES Have some enDearing trait. But NONE is Like dick the terriBLe, the Biggest cLOWN in the Line.

dick knew he was near camp and quitting time, and nothing under god's BLue sky was going to sLow him up.

*H*ARRY BAUM, ONE OF OUR Indian guides, swung himself around in his saddle, took a hurried backward glance up the steep, narrow trail, and shouted, "Get out of the way. *Get off the trail!*"

His hunter, Joe Knot of New York, took one look and yelled, "Get go'n. Those horns'll kill you."

Our wrangler plunged his mount over the edge of the trail, shouting a dire warning: "Scram, you guys. Dick's com'n!"

My husband, Louis, and I looked up and saw Dick, a 1,500-pound bay gelding, pause on the skyline and calmly survey the mad scramble of men and horses below him. Silhouetted on his top packs were a set of 68-inch moose antlers and a jagged pair of caribou antlers with double shovels. Dick was no fool. He knew he was nearing camp and quitting time, and nothing under God's blue sky was going to slow him down.

He came down the trail at full speed. A timid packhorse lingered too long and received a sharp jab in the flank. She squealed and plunged off the trail. Dick galloped past her and slammed to a halt beside the huddled horses waiting to be led across the river. Dick gave a whinny and stared at the water. Louis grinned at me and said, "Sounds like Dick's saying, 'Come on boys, follow me. I'll find a crossing.'" Sure enough, Dick took off with the other packhorses stringing along behind him.

Louis and I dug in our spurs, swung around the line of horses, and found a shallow riffle 500 yards upstream. We turned in our saddles to signal the two wranglers to drive them across. Instead we stopped, frozen in our saddles. Standing on top of the biggest beaver house in the Yukon was Dick, and the deepest spot in the whole Wind River was in front of him. Dick had found his own crossing.

*W*hen I left my clerking job in the State House in Olympia, Washington, for a big-game hunt to the Yukon in 1951, I fell in love with the Yukon and Louis J. Brown, my outfitter-guide. I married

both of them in 1953. My boss, H. D. VanEaton, was skeptical. "Can there really be human beings who think happiness ever after is found in a log cabin in a snowfield?" he asked me. I'm one of those idiots who do, and I moved from Olympia to Mayo Landing, a log-cabin town about 247 miles north of Whitehorse.

Now, in 1955, I was tagging along behind my husband while he guided American hunters. Louis had taught me what to do in case a grizzly bear charged me, but I wasn't prepared for Dick, by all odds the biggest clown in our string of packhorses.

Louis and I were trying to find a shallow ford to cross Yukon's Wind River, which flowed at the foot of the trail, when we heard the commotion.

Louis stood in his stirrups. "Get that damn horse off that beaver house," he yelled to the men.

I gnawed my lip and wailed, "Oh Louis, Louis, he's going to jump."

"Every packhorse in the outfit is going to follow him too," Louis groaned.

"Dick'll drown them all. If they get into the beavers' food cache of cut willows, they'll tangle and that's the finish of them."

Joe Knot galloped up. "Dick, Dick, don't," he pleaded, "you've got my bed on you."

"Bed?" his brother Paul scoffed. "He's got $20,000 worth of my camera equipment on him."

"That's the orneriest, most cussed horse I ever saw," Louis said. "I feel like shooting him." It was about the 20th time on this hunt I'd heard Dick threatened with quick execution.

Guides and wranglers raced ahead, swinging their hats and yelling. Dick looked around. Louis stormed, "Now just look at that. Look at that fool horse, will you? He knows better." Dick stretched his neck low over the water and bent his knees.

Louis bought Dick from the government in 1952 for $25. The Indians had been hauling timber with him. They used to overload the sleigh deliberately just to watch Dick balk, back up and sit down on the lumber. He stubbornly refused to haul such heavy loads. It struck the Indians as funny to see a big, old, shaggy horse sitting on the lumber with his hairy lower lip drooping and quivering with indignation. The Indians rolled in the snow with laughter and thought it a huge joke.

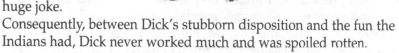

Consequently, between Dick's stubborn disposition and the fun the Indians had, Dick never worked much and was spoiled rotten.

Every winter, Louis and Dick had a standing battle over fences. There was to be a New Year's dance in Mayo to celebrate the arrival of 1955. Louis worked all day reinforcing the fence around the haystack. Late that afternoon, he came into the house beaming with satisfaction. "This is one time that old codger isn't going to go through the fence while we're gone," he told me. "I braced it with eight-inch logs."

We had a wonderful time at the dance that night until we arrived home in the wee hours and our car's headlights swept across the barn lot and picked up two bright green eyes shining from the top of the haystack. Louis slammed on the brakes. "Now look at that son of a gun," he said. "How on earth did he get through that fence? I'll bet he's chewed up a month's rations." Dick and Louis spent the rest of the winter in dispute over the fence around that haystack, and by spring it was still a tie.

In July, we started planning for the hunting season. "I'll be blamed if I'm going to take Dick on this hunt," Louis announced. "Remember what he did last year?"

I remembered, and I felt my head. "I've had a bump on top ever since he crashed the cook tent," I recalled. "That ridgepole made me see a million sputniks in orbit."

"That was bad," Louis nodded sympathetically, "but it was downright embarrassing when Dick stuck his old Roman nose through the hunters' tent and chewed up all their cigarettes."

"You're not taking Dick then?" I asked.

"We're going to have some peace. Dick's staying home."

Sometimes you think you've eliminated one source of trouble only to run into another, and that's particularly true with a string of packhorses. Early that fall, we were getting our pack train loaded. Equipment was piled high. Wranglers rushed to cinch packsaddles. Guides ran back and forth sorting packs.

Someone yelled in alarm, and I looked to see why. I felt like fainting. A tiny three-year-old had Trigger's hind leg clutched in her little arms. "Nice horsy, nice horsy," she gurgled. Trigger is the only horse in the outfit that really kicks.

What could I do ? If I grabbed the child I'd most likely scare the horse. Neither could I yell at him. Thrusting my hand into my pocket, I pulled out a candy bar. Quickly kneeling, I held it out to the child. "Do you like candy? Do you like candy ?" I cooed.

She held out a hand for it but still clung to Trigger with the other. I watched Trigger's every twitch. I held the candy closer. "Come and get it," I told her.

She let go and came running to me. Weakly, I gave her the candy. Had it been a guide or a wrangler, Trigger would have kicked his head off. I ordered all children to stay back of the rope fence and issued warnings of good spankings for children found among the horses. Kids are just as fascinated by our pack string as I always was by the Ringling Brothers Circus back in Seattle when I was growing up.

I walked over to tell Louis about the narrow escape and stopped dead in my tracks at the sight of him packing a big, shaggy bay. He gave the horse a pat. "Dick, you old son of a gun," he said, "you're the only horse in the outfit that can stand up under this load."

"Why Louis, I thought you weren't going to take Dick."

"Well I wasn't," Louis grinned sheepishly. "But I forgot I'd promised to take this hammer drill out to that old prospector on Moosehide Creek, and Dick's the only horse that can pack it."

"I suppose I'll get some more bumps on my head," I sighed.

The packhorses strung out single file as we left the end of the dirt road and started up the hunting trail. Baldy bared his big, yellow teeth and sank them into Donna's flank. She kicked and squealed but let Baldy have his favorite place in line. Then she kicked Jim in the jaw for her own special place. A shrill squeal sounded far behind us, and a runted 1½ -year-old colt named Copper came tearing up the trail to catch up. He looked so small and helpless, I promised myself I'd look after him. I soon changed my mind. With head and tail up, Copper flashed past me, and my mount, Shorty, gave a surprised grunt, slid back on his haunches and almost upset me. Louis looked back and laughed. "Shorty has two hoofprints where Copper kicked him. But don't worry, I don't think he's hurt bad," he said.

About 100 yards to the right, a herd of caribou trotted past. Copper squealed and took after them as if they were long-lost relatives. The wranglers gave chase and herded him back into line.

After traveling a mile or two, the packhorses settled down, pretty much satisfied with their places. The horses were slick and fat even though the temperature had dropped to 74 below during the previous winter. It was well worth the effort of putting up hay. We make a living with our horses during the hunting season, and we don't let them starve during the winter.

Every horse of ours has some endearing trait. Put Donna on the trail of a lost horse, and she'll track him down every time. Dan, the big blond, kicks every drunk that comes near him. Kate, the gray with scars made by wolf fangs, has game eyes. She can spot a moose or a grizzly miles away. Harry Baum, who claims her for his saddle horse, says, "She sure let me know when she see moose or something. She twitch her ear and look. Good horse." And so on down the line, ending with Dick the Terrible.

Six days later we arrived at our main camp, situated three miles below Three River Lake on the Wind River. The Wind flows into the Peel River, which, in turn, empties into the Mackenzie River about 90 miles from the Arctic Ocean. The drill had been safely delivered, and our hunters were anxious to start hunting. I overheard Paul Knot talking to Louis. "Now, Lou," he said, "I brought a lot of expensive cameras and equipment. I'd like you to put them on the safest horse you've got."

"That's easy," Louis said. "Dick, that big bay over there, is smart. You never catch him stuck in the mud. He's like an amphibious tank."

"Will he buck?"

"He's too lazy."

"You consider him absolutely reliable?"

"Absolutely. He's the best horse in the outfit."

I never realized before how much Louis loved that old scalawag.

We started out the next day with Dick placidly striding along under a load of camera equipment, two cases of rum, most of the things the hunters considered valuable, plus their beds. There wasn't room for a bottle of imported whisky, so Joe stuck it into one of Tootsie's top packs. Tootsie also carried our flat-top, folding dining-room table. She hated it and rammed it against every tree she could get to. She was trying to reach an old spruce when she ran into a fresh grizzly track. She screamed, pawed the air, whirled and bucked viciously. The two top packs flew off, and the third tangled in the cinch rope and wound around Tootsie's leg. Every time she kicked, the bag flew into the air. Before it could crash to the ground, Tootsie let fly with another kick and up sailed the bag again. Joe rode up and said, "That's the bag with the whisky in it. What a cocktail shaker! If I only had some shaved ice."

I wasn't so optimistic. "If that bottle isn't broken to smithereens, I'll eat my hat," I told Joe.

The wranglers caught Tootsie and then handed something to Joe. Joe walked over to me, jerked my hat off and said, "Start eating." The bottle was intact.

Though Tootsie failed to break the bottle, she succeeded nicely with my table. During dinner, Joe lost his plate of soup down one hole and a pot of beans disappeared down another.

The next morning, as we were climbing a pass, I heard the wranglers cursing in exasperation. I turned to look and saw Dick standing alone on a narrow ledge. Dick loved scenery. Lush grass grew on the ledge, but Dick kept gazing out over the vast valley below. He was driving the wranglers wild. The whole pack train was out of sight, but Dick still stood looking. Finally, a well-aimed rock broke the spell, and Dick trotted to catch up so he wouldn't miss the next good view.

The trail was getting steeper and narrower, and I watched Dick as he edged his way around the pack string to his favorite place, back of Lonny Johnny, the lead guide. Louis rode up beside me. "Look at that, now just look at that," he groaned.

"What's the matter?" I asked.

"Well just look at that mess up there."

I took another look up the trail. Dick was lying down in the middle of it. He was like a cork in a bottle. None of the horses could get past him, and they were squealing and kicking. We crawled over boulders and around horses to get to him. It was mad-dening to see Dick calmly reclined and nibbling on the succulent grass at the edge of a trickle of glacier water. Louis let out a hissing breath. "Now if that isn't the craziest trick," he moaned. "Harry, we'll have to unload him."

Harry Baum jerked a rope, then grinned. "Boss, him smart horse. Cinch rope broke. He no buck. He lie down."

We crossed the high part of the pass and started down. It was steep, and Shorty, my horse, stopped. I yelled and pounded him, but he wouldn't move. Harry, riding behind, said, "Him saddle loose."

Sure enough, when I got off, the saddle did too. For the rest of the day, I marveled at the wonderful intelligence of animals. But I vaguely wondered if Shorty really was that smart.

About 100 yards farther down the trail, he proved to me he was. He stopped again. I quickly checked my saddle. It was tight. I nudged and coaxed. Shorty stood in stubborn silence. I tried to lead him, but Shorty wouldn't lead. He kept looking back, so I looked to see if his hind legs were caught. Seeing nothing wrong, I wondered what to do next. Shorty never stopped looking back. I turned and saw that the packhorse following us was carrying a spare saddle and it had swung under his belly. At my call, the wranglers came and fixed the saddle. When I remounted, Shorty took off at a trot.

Now we rode into the main valley of the Bonnet Plume River. The trail wound 50 feet above the water. Here and there, the banks had caved in, and we had to make wide detours. Dick had lagged and was just in front of me. Seeing another cave-in just ahead, I tried to swing in front of Dick to make him go around, but Dick's mind was made up and he went straight ahead. He galloped past me and jumped. In horror, I watched the soft ground disintegrate under him and heard him scream as he went down the steep bank. Paul, wild with concern, leaped from his mount and skidded down the bank. He was followed by both wranglers, one with a gun. The wrangler reasoned that no horse could land on a pile of rocks without breaking a leg. It seemed as though Dick was falling for hours, but he landed on some soft ground between three boulders. What's more, he landed on his feet. The men didn't catch him until he had climbed back onto the trail. Louis shook his head in disbelief.

We anxiously gathered around as Paul carefully checked his camera equipment. At last, he looked up rather dazed. "Dick must be enchanted. Not a thing's broken," he said.

That night, the northern lights gleamed cold and hard, and the moon bathed the whole landscape in bleak, eerie light. At midnight, hoofs pounded on the frost-hardened ground. I stuck my head out under the tent wall and saw a horse coming our way at a gallop. Trailing behind it was the shadowy form of a wolf. They came closer. I recognized the horse. "Louis, wake up," I shouted. "A wolf is going to eat Dick."

"I doubt it," Louis grunted. "Dick's too tough. Go back to sleep."

At dawn I staggered sleepily to the kitchen tent. Louis greeted me with, "Can you guess what Dick did last night?"

"Yes, he kept me awake banging around camp."

"He tipped the cache over and ate up the oats, and that's not all. He chewed up the hunters' washing."

While getting breakfast that morning, I planned ahead for lunch and put enough extra potatoes on the stove so I'd have some for a salad. Suddenly, the tent jerked and wobbled. Here comes the ridgepole, I thought. Instead, there was a rattling by the stove behind me. I turned in time to see Dick's teeth crunch down on a potato. That potato evidently tasted so good to Dick that he ignored the crash of a frying pan on his cranium. He went on chomping. I called to Louis, "Shag this beast out of my kitchen before I take my .270 to him."

By now the hunters had their sheep, caribou and moose, and there was only one bear to go. The pack train was winding down the trail headed for an old caribou kill near a lake. Louis told Paul, "It's been two weeks since you shot that caribou. Might be a grizzly on it now."

"Could be," he said. "I can't go home without one."

So Louis and Paul left us to look at the carcass, while the pack train continued on to the next camp.

Dick and I were fighting for the honor of leading the outfit when I remembered that Dick knew where the next camp was and I didn't. The rest of the hunters, their guides and the wranglers were singing happily as they trailed along behind the pack string. I let Dick pass and kept away from the wicked caribou and moose horns he was carrying.

Dick had just swung around me when a grizzly bear walked out from behind a knoll. Dick took one look and whirled in midair. For a moment, he seemed to hang suspended, and I saw those massive horns above me. I kicked Shorty, but not in time. When Dick came down there was a sharp pain and a tearing sound at the back of my jacket. Knowing that the first thing a horse does when he sees a bear

dick took one Look at the grizzly, whirled in midair,
and tore back up the trail.

is to buck, I grabbed all available leather. Shorty and I tore back up the trail right on Dick's tail. Seeing us bearing down on them at such frightful speed, the rest of the horses turned and bolted. The singing ended abruptly.

Seeing the commotion, Louis and Paul came galloping back. We rode on toward camp and were almost there when Dick decided to use the beaver house for a diving board, as I mentioned earlier. The wranglers yelled and shouted, but it did no good. Dick stretched his neck out farther over the water. I closed my eyes and heard a loud splash. "And I trusted that horse," Paul groaned. "Everything's ruined now."

Chief and Jim, two normally sane packhorses, jumped after Dick. Chief went into a panic. He was afraid to swim across, but he couldn't climb back onto the beaver house. He started swimming upstream, then got tangled in the beavers' cache of cut willows. Struggling, he freed himself and floated downstream. He tried to climb the beaver house again, but fell back into the water and floundered among the willows. Louis and Harry plunged into the water to rescue him. The horse was frantic and getting dangerous to help. "Get on that log and hold his head up," Louis yelled to Harry. "He's going to drown. He's got his foot caught in a loose cinch."

Louis snatched his knife from his belt and went under. He slashed the cinches and rolled the pack off the exhausted horse. The aching cold of that subarctic river was taking the horse's strength. Chief swam feebly across, joined the other two horses on the bank and stood there shaking.

Dick stood in a puddle of blood. He had cut one of his front feet on the rocks and could barely limp to camp. The wranglers hurriedly unpacked him, and Paul, greatly agitated, dived into the duffel bags after his photographic gear. We waited anxiously while he inspected everything carefully. At last, he turned to Louis, grinned and said, "It's a good thing you gave me those plastic bags and rubber bands. Not a thing got wet."

The next morning, before we said goodbye to the hunters, Joe led Dick over to the tents. He put his battered felt hat on Dick's head and stuck a pipe in the horse's mouth. "Take our picture," he said to Paul.

Sixteen more hunters came and went that season, and at last we headed for home. Dick's foot had become infected, and he was still limping and had thinned down a lot. We didn't pack him. The horses seemed to know we were going home, and their daily mileage increased. Every day, the snow crept farther down the mountains, and as the horses waded the creeks, ice froze on their tails and bellies. It was time to leave the high country. It felt good to be heading south, but little did we dream that we were also headed for the most spectacular stunt Dick ever pulled on us.

I was riding Bunny, a sure-footed mare with large feet. Still, Louis was afraid she might fall on the ice-sheathed trail. "You better get off here and lead Bunny," he told me.

I got off, took two steps and fell flat on my face. The breath was knocked out of me. The packhorses slammed into Bunny. But Bunny didn't let them by. She kicked and squealed and held them back until Louis could reach me and fling me back into the saddle. "Those crazy horses headed for home would have smashed you flat if it hadn't been for a good horse," Louis told me later.

Late the next afternoon, we came to a deep river crossing and unpacked the horses. They'd swim while we paddled equipment across in a rubber boat. Harry looked at Dick and said, "Don't know. Foot bad. Maybe him can't swim. He maybe weak."

"I think the current is too swift for him," Louis agreed.

I was worried sick. Half the fun in life would be gone if anything happened to Dick. "What can we do?" I asked anxiously.

"Give him a pair of water wings," Louis grinned.

"Oh, don't be funny."

"I mean it."

"Where would you get water wings here in the muskeg?"

"I'm going to use our air mattresses."

"Air mattresses? Louis Brown, you're crazy."

"Just watch me float that old duffer across."

While the boys blew up our air mattresses, the horses milled around at the edge of the river. Even though Dick was weak, he wasn't going to be left behind. Harry caught his halter. "Wait, you bag of bones," he said. "You go across like white man."

The men used two cinch ropes to lash an air mattress on each side of the horse. Dick looked like some creature from Mars. All that showed of him was a straggly tail, a homely mug and four knotty knees.

We drove the horses into the water. Dick hesitated while sizing up the queer rig encasing him. He looked up. The other horses were starting to swim. Dick gave a whinny and plunged in. To our glee, the air mattresses floated him high in the water. Dick had so much buoyancy, he rode the water as though he had a caribou's hollow hair. Harry slapped his knee, roared with mirth and chortled, "He like motorboat."

Dick was going so fast he plowed right through the other horses. Some went under, others scattered. They snorted with fright and swam in every direction—anything to get away from that frightful monster. Dick kept buzzing high among them. "Go on, you old fool," we yelled at him. "Get out of there."

Finally, Dick swam past the other horses and headed for the opposite bank. We sighed with relief, but when Dick got to shore he looked around and saw that he was alone. He gave a lonesome whinny and jumped back in. "Him drown them all," Harry yelled.

Lonny Johnny grabbed his gun. "Shoot air mattress?" he asked, looking at Louis.

The rest of the horses were in mortal terror of Dick. Some looked as if they were sinking. Lonny aimed.

"Stop," Louis yelled. "You think I want to sleep on the ground the rest of this trip?"

By screaming and throwing rocks, we finally got Dick turned around, and soon afterward the whole bunch reached shore. We jumped into the rubber boat and furiously paddled across. We had to catch Dick before he could put a hole in our mattresses.

When he awoke the next morning, Louis groaned. "I'm stiff," he said. "There's a leak in my mattress."

This was our last day on the trail, and the horses seemed to fly. Even Dick revived enough to carry the moose rack. Eventually, we left the trail and struck the dirt road leading to Keno. Rounding a bend, we saw two unsteady customers coming out the door of the Silver Queen Hotel's beer parlor.

Dick galloped ahead of us. As he drew near, the two drunks clutched each other. "My God, that horse's grown horns," one of them shouted. They fled back to the safety of the parlor.

Finally, we were home, and Louis was laughing when he took the moose antlers off Dick's back. "Well, you old son of a gun," he said, "another season's over. Now go prop yourself up against a haystack and keep alive until next year."

STAG PARTY - One reason the first stocking of chukar partridge in Utah back in 1932 failed to take hold was that all of the 100 or so birds purchased from an Eastern game farm turned out to be males. - Casey Brown, PROVO (UT) HERALD.

INNOCENT VICTIM - An archer hunting deer from a tree stand who couldn't resist a shot at a passing mama bear hit her right in the fanny with a blunt (a target arrow that can't penetrate); whereupon she whirled around and swatted her dutifully following cub 20 feet into the brush. - Pick McCune, DALLAS (TX) TIMES HERALD.

DRY RUN - When Harold Lamson of Williamstown drove his cattle into the barn he found one extra animal. A deer that had been feeding with the cows went in with them. Lamson didn't try to milk it. - P. G. Angwin, BARRE (VT) TIMES.

taLL
BUt
SHORt

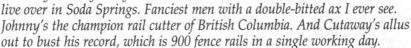

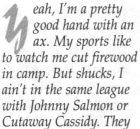

eah, I'm a pretty good hand with an ax. My sports like to watch me cut firewood in camp. But shucks, I ain't in the same league with Johnny Salmon or Cutaway Cassidy. They live over in Soda Springs. Fanciest men with a double-bitted ax I ever see. Johnny's the champion rail cutter of British Columbia. And Cutaway's allus out to bust his record, which is 900 fence rails in a single working day.

Well, one day last spring Cutaway gets up real early, eats three moose steaks with a gallon of tea and says to himself, "This is the day! This is the day I bust Johnny's record and set a new one that no one will ever beat."

He shoulders his razor-sharp ax at dawn and goes into the best patch of rail poplars in the whole country. He slams the ax into a big tree whilst he takes off his coat and shirt, then grabs it again and soon has the chips flying so thick they darken the sun.

Well sir, Cutaway works all day—even through the lunch hour—and he figures he's good for at least a hundred rails an hour. So at 4:30 he knocks off, figuring he's got Johnny's record well beat. But when he piles and counts the rails he finds he's cut only 872!

He's just sick with disappointment. But there's nothing left to do but go home, so he starts to put on his shirt and coat. And, by golly, what does he see? Why, the bit of his ax—still stuck in the big tree. No wonder he hadn't been able to beat Johnny's record. He'd been cutting fence rails all day with an ax handle!

George W. Renner

"stay with it boy— he can't last much longer
with that net around him."

"quick, john! he's pointing at something."

working the lever of his shiny new rifle, he spilled out unexploded cartridges while his guide nearly had a fit.

Buck Fever?

by Gordon Graham

COOL, CALM, COLLECTED? NOT SO'S you'd NOTICE it! AND if tHE DAY ever comes WHEN my puLse DOESN'T RACE, i'm THROUGH!

AYBE YOU HANKER TO BECOME so proficient in your hunting that, with the nonchalance of a Dan'l Boone, you can yawn, scratch, flick a fleck of dandruff from your shoulder as you raise your rifle, draw a bead three and a half inches back of the first rib of a deer and squeeze off in the best target-range style. But if I ever get to that height of cool serenity in the presence of game I'll give up hunting entirely!

I'll venture a guess that those guys who are so expert that they beef when their shot is a quarter inch off the center of the brisket would give a purty could they regain just once some of the wild thrill they experienced when they saw the first rabbit or squirrel tumble to their shot.

Every once in a while I get to feeling a little blah-zay myself, like I'd like to breathe on my nails and polish 'em on my coat lapel before each shot. And then something happens that jerks me back to the reality of my eternal dubbism—to the realization that Ol' Debbil Buck Fever is just around the corner and ready to send me into a tizzy at any moment.

I got one of these come-uppances just a while back. I am a reason-ably diligent devotee of varmint shooting. I own a rifle in one of the hot wildcat calibers, handload for it and even make my own jacketed bullets. I am, furthermore, the proprietor of a bench rest, a spotting scope, micrometer calipers, a neck reamer, a case gauge and a fine library of groups that measure considerably better than minute of angle.

Furthermore, I manage to get in a considerable amount of actual varmint shooting as well as bench-rest time. This particular season I had accounted for more than 80 chucks and several bushels of crows, so I was properly inflated for the sticking I got one afternoon.

The Ever-Loving, who has accused me of putting a dash of gun oil behind each ear before dressing for an evening out, accompanied me to a nearby chuck pasture and was a delighted witness to the down-fall of the mighty hunter.

Vexed by a Vixen

She did her level best to follow my whispered admonitions about keeping low, walking silently, staying behind me and keeping mum as we tiptoed to the edge of the wide creek valley behind Howard Cain's barn. The little alfalfa patch stretched from a point 50 feet down the slope in front of us across a couple of hundred yards to the brushy, weed-grown creek bed on the other side of the valley.

I first scanned the upper end of the alfalfa through the 8X Unertl scope, then stepped from behind the little sycamore tree where I was crouched, in order to see the rest of the field. At that moment there was a rustle in the weeds along the near fence and a huge red fox burst into the open and lit out across the field, seeming to float like a toy balloon, her fluffy tail riding grandly in her wake.

So unexpected was the appearance of the big vixen that I forgot something I knew perfectly well—namely, that she'd probably stop for an instant before entering the heavy cover across the field, and that if I were in good position and ready I'd undoubtedly get a nice standing shot at perhaps 200 yards. Instead of waiting, I swung up the rifle, flicked the safety off and tried to hold that bounding critter in the field of the big scope.

The shot was two feet wide, and the fox really went into high gear, bounding into the weeds across the field before I could reload.

About that time I did what I should have done in the first place—dropped to the prone position, and hissed to the Better Half to do likewise. There was just a bare chance the fox might bob into sight at some other point and afford another chance.

Scarcely had my elbows touched the ground, however, when another and quite different fox bobbed up, 100 yards along the fence from where the first one had disappeared. I swung wildly over to this second target and jerked the trigger, knowing as the shot sounded that I'd pulled off. Before the echoes died away the first fox was back in the alfalfa field and running like blue blazes down the fence, heading to my left.

Ever try to swing on a fast-running target from the prone position? I mean running so fast that you have to walk on your elbows to follow the critter? You'd be surprised what variations on the standard prone position you can assume in two seconds.

That Old, Old Feeling

I squibbed off three times as the fox dashed down the field, and never touched a hair. When the fox had disappeared, I realized for the first time what a pitiable condition I was in. Only 30 seconds had gone by, but I was like a chap who's just run a mile on a hot day with a 100-pound sack of black-eyed peas on his head. My pulse was pounding, sweat poured into my eyes, my breath was labored and trembling. Any practiced mortician would have licked his chops in anticipation, could he have seen me at that moment.

"What's the matter, Boonie—got a little touch of the buck?" My War Department chuckled as she patted into place a lock of hair that had been displaced by the muzzle blasts.

"Nah," I answered, and nonchalantly picked up three or four empty cases, stuck one of them in my mouth and attempted to light it. "The field of the scope was stuck. I mean—aw, skip it!"

Later, having analyzed the incident in my basement laboratory, I came to the conclusion that, though it had been embarrassing in the extreme to put on this kind of performance in the presence of a witness, I wouldn't have missed it for the world. If that wild-and-woolly, pulse-pounding feeling ever goes away and leaves me, somebody else can have my guns.

Bill Tries a Place Kick

The late Bill Blake, who operated a Michigan fishing and hunting establishment, was a walking library of stories about duffers and their reactions to the first sight of a buck. Bill himself never quite got over the moon-eyed madness that infects the hunter. He endeared himself to me beyond all description when I downed my first buck. Scarcely had my five-shot barrage ceased to rattle the leaves when I became conscious of Bill's voice booming from the other side of the little ridge where we were hunting.

"Keep shooting! Keep shooting!" he bellowed as he came plowing down through the brush like a runaway truck. "Keep shoot—wup, so ya got him," he said as he slid to a halt beside me and spotted the buck kicking on the ground less than 100 feet away.

"Now keep back, boy," he cautioned. "Keep away from him till you're sure he's done for." And so saying, he circled up to the stern of the eight-pointer and dealt him a hearty kick in the rump, at the same time receiving a resounding whack on the shin from one of the buck's flailing rear hoofs.

The shock of the kick and the pain of his barked shin apparently reminded Bill that he too was a little excited, and he later confessed to me that he'd had a touch of the meemies.

That same year I saw an acquaintance of mine from the Hoosier state, a big and brawny broth of a lad, down his first buck. Whereas I had just stood and trembled and sweated upon bagging my initial specimen, Clyde exploded into furious physical action as The Buck invaded his metabolism.

CLYÐE GAVE A WHOOP, THREW THE GUN AWAY AND STARTEÐ ÐOWNHILL, WITH THE FORKHORN'S LEGS STILL KICKING.

Standing atop a steep, timbered ridge, Clyde swung his borrowed rifle with professional aplomb as a fat forkhorn, chased up by some other hunters, went bounding by him at 50 feet. With a single shot Clyde broke the little fellow's neck and the deer somersaulted into the dry leaves, kicking his last.

Clyde didn't even wait for the kicking to stop. I have the word of eyewitnesses and Clyde's own somewhat confused account that, as the buck went head over heels, Clyde emitted a whoop, threw the rifle away, bounded forward, seized one of the forked antlers and made off down the steep hillside, dragging the buck behind him while its hind legs still thrashed wildly.

A quarter of a mile straight down the steep hillside on the run and then across the clearing went the hunter, never stopping until he sank, sobbing for breath, red-faced and wobbly-kneed, on the running board of his car. Other hunters, coming along in the wake of the tornado, found Clyde sitting glassy-eyed, still clutching the antler in one huge fist.

On another occasion I stood less than 100 yards from a hunter and a guide who were suddenly confronted by a buster with a rack of fabulous proportions. The buck stepped out of the brush so close that a fair-to-middling tobacco chewer stocked up with Brown's Mule could have spit in his eye.

Instead of whipping his shiny new rifle to his shoulder, the hunter just held it under one arm and worked the lever six or seven times, spinning out a series of unexploded cartridges. The buck stood there until the last cartridge had kicked up the snow, then turned and walked with dignity out of sight. The hunter went on rattling the action of the empty rifle, while his unarmed guide hovered on the verge of apoplexy.

Another hunter I knew got an easy, open, standing shot at close range but pointed his gun at the sky and touched it off, thus assuring the rapid departure of the deer. He watched it bound away, never making a move to reload or even to point his rifle in the general direction of the buck.

A million such yarns, most of them true, are heard around the nation's deer camps. Even upland hunters experience much the same feeling each autumn when they flush their first covey of quail or when the season's first pheasant goes whirring skyward.

Whether it's deer or doves, I like that shortness of breath when game heaves into view. You can keep your cool, calm, and collected characters. Just gimme a shot of that heady stuff, that gosh-all-hemlock, here-we-go feeling.

You don't need to be a Daniel Boone to enjoy it. It's dividends for dubs, buck fever is. I like it!

taLL
BUt
SHORt

Sure I'm choosy about who I drink with. Pays to be. Tell you why. One time, way back, I done a spell of prospecting up north. Got awful lonely, all by myself in them woods, so when I come across a stray grizzly cub one day I took her home. We got along fine. She learned to set up to the table and eat her grub off a plate just as good as me. I called her Rowdy.

When the blueberries got ripe, Rowdy and me picked ourselves a crop. Then I made some wine in a big barrel I had. Turned out fine. Me and Rowdy used to set around evenings and drink it, me talking and her listening. Come winter, she dug herself in under the cabin and I went back to town with my poke. Didn't go up to the cabin again for three years.

When I did go back, I stopped off to see a friend. He told me that a big grizzly had taken over my place. That's Rowdy, I figured. He gave me a bottle of wine and I went on to the cabin.

Sure enough, there was the bear—she musta run 1,200 pounds—at the front door. She picked up my scent right off and stood looking at me. "Rowdy!" I says. She cocked her head and started for me. Tell you, I was scared! When she was 10 foot away I held out the bottle. She took it, gave it a tilt and swallowed the wine—just like I taught her. Then she took me by the arm and escorted me into the cabin. You know what? There stood the old barrel, filled to the brim with wine. Rowdy got a cup off the shelf, dipped it full and handed it to me. Smarter'n scat! But that ain't what floored me.

While I was drinking the wine I took a look outdoors. And out of the woods come two grizzly cubs—each carrying a bucket of blueberries.

William E. Johnson

"someone told me a pheasant will do that—come right at you."

as the youngest, i was elected to push him off the tree limb.

Coon Hunting

by Ray Beck

COONS merely humiliate cocky men, but an arrogant dog that tangles with one can lose face literally.

PAPPY NEVER CARED TOO MUCH for Uncle Frank. In the first place, he was Mom's relative; in the second, he was always bragging about something. One time it would be about how much money he was making. Next it would be his '26 Buick touring car.

Now it was about his new dog, a German shepherd. For an hour he entertained us with tales of the ferocity and fighting ability of the breed. As time went on, the stories became wilder and harder for me to believe, but Pappy apparently was swallowing them all, hook, line and sinker.

"They ought to be deadly on coons," Pappy ventured.

"Coons," snorted Uncle Frank. "Why, one bite and it would be the end of the coon. Did I tell you about the German shepherd that killed two wolves?"

"Twice," I said. I might have added that I'd seen the movie too, but Pappy gave me a dirty look, so I kept quiet.

"I'll tell you what we'll do," said Pappy enthusiastically, as though the idea had just struck him. "We'll take your dog and Old Blue out tonight. Old Blue can still trail all right, but his teeth aren't so good anymore. We'll let Blue tree the coon, and then tie him up and shake the coon down for your dog to kill."

Too late, Uncle Frank saw the trap he'd talked himself into. He must have taken some consolation from the thought that his dog could handle two like Old Blue—and Old Blue killed coons—but it was noticeable that his boasting was considerably toned down for the next couple of hours.

about 10 o'clock we got our lights and dogs and started. Pappy put a jug of cider in the back of his hunting coat in case he got thirsty. I took the .22 in case the coon took refuge on a treetop too big to climb, and Uncle Frank carried the ax because, as Pappy said later, he would hate to trust him with the jug.

In those days, coons weren't as plentiful in western Pennsylvania as they are now. Sometimes we'd have to walk all the way to the Clarion River to get one started, but that night we were lucky. We'd only gone about four miles when Old Blue struck a track. He took up Smith Run toward Huckleberry Ridge, turned west near the Cobler Farm and headed back toward Canoe Creek, finally treeing on a white oak just across the creek from Japes Spring.

While not a den tree in the strict sense of the word, the oak was hollow, and there was a hole a small coon could squeeze into. We had lost a coon at this tree the season before, and I was afraid it might happen again, but I needn't have worried. No amount of dieting would have enabled this particular coon to get into that hole.

it dug its front claws into the dog's face to steady itself
and started working its hind feet.

It was 20 feet to the first limbs, but from there the climbing wouldn't be bad, so Pappy cut a sapling and leaned it against the oak for a ladder. As the youngest, I was elected to climb. They gave me a boost as high as they could reach, and I didn't have much trouble shinnying up to where I could reach a limb.

Pappy tossed me a stick with a fork on the end, and I started beating the limb the coon was on. Sometimes they'll jump when you do that, but this one made me climb out and push him off.

Old Blue was bawling his head off at missing all the fun. Uncle Frank's dog made a dive at the coon, which was lying on its back, and then he started bawling too. I don't think he bit the coon at all, but there wasn't any doubt that the coon got its teeth onto the end of the shepherd's nose. It dug its front claws into the dog's face to steady itself and started working its hind feet. At every kick the hair flew. Right then the shepherd lost all interest in coon hunting. Uncle Frank was dancing around them waving the ax.

When the shepherd finally threw the coon off, Pappy was laughing so hard he could scarcely loosen Old Blue. When he got around to it, Old Blue caught the coon within 100 yards, and by the time we arrived it was all over.

The shepherd had made the same mistake a lot of inexperienced dogs make. He had tackled the coon while it was on its back. Grabbing a coon by the belly is about like grabbing a buzz saw. . . .

taLL
But
SHORT

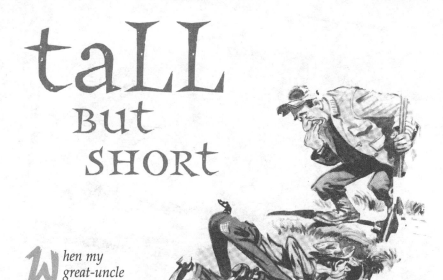

When my great-uncle Blodgett passed on to glory I heired one of his dogs, a cross between a beagle and a dachshund, and it turned out to be a mighty useful critter, cause it could go into holes after foxes, rabbits, woodchucks and suchlike. Always managed to wiggle its way in and out. All but one time.

This time it chased a rabbit into a six-inch culvert that run under the road. The rabbit came out the other end, all right, but Yardstick (that's what I called the dog) got stuck in the pipe. I was fit to be tied. Short of digging up the road and busting open the culvert I didn't see how I was going to get him out. And my, how he howled and howled.

Then I thought of Stringbean Sammis. Stringbean was the skinniest man I ever seen. When he swallowed a black-eyed pea, you could follow its course all the way down his gullet. So I went over and got Stringbean and told him my trouble. "Your problem is solved," he said. "I'll go through that culvert and push Yardstick out ahead of me."

Well, he went into the culvert, all right, and a couple of minutes later he came out the other end. But no dog!

"Hey, what's the matter?" I asks.

"Ain't no dog in there," he says.

"There sure is!" I says. And just at that moment Yardstick starts howling again in the culvert.

"Well, I'll be durned!" says Stringbean. "Guess I'll have to go through again. I must have passed him the first time!"

Rodney Douglass

i peeked from shelter after Queenie's first howl to see
if she was dead or alive.

Sucker Bait

by Paul Miller

though my old wounds twitch at the
thought, wasp nests hold wonderful
fish lures. you take it from there.

·

WASPS. THAT IS OUR TEXT FOR today. And my message from Georgia is that wasp grubs are panfish bait worthy of the crippling wounds you may get robbing their cradle. Wasps do have both mothers and fathers, you'll discover, and their normal, tranquil state is fighting mad.

On a hook, any wasp grub has a caviar rating for the bluegill or red-breasted bream, the shiner, the speckled, blue or mud cat, warmouth perch, sucker and—sometimes—the largemouth bass.

So, when I was a boy and we felt the hungry urge for a fish fry, our first step was in the direction of wasp country. This may be anywhere from the barn eaves to the bulrushes in a swamp. Usually it's near water, for there grows more of the pulpwood they need to manufacture, in their personal mills, the paper for their nests. Except for the low-minded yellow jacket, they build their nests in trees, high or low, attached to a bush, hidden in a clump of blackberry briers or in a mixed mass of blackberry canes and bulrushes. Having more contempt than fear of man, the devils are also likely to build under barn or shed eaves.

That makes it simple: just reach up with a long fishing pole, rake the nest loose and make sure you are behind the barn before it hits the ground. I mean a long cane pole, and stay near the building's corner in opening negotiations. Finally, don't stand there poking at the nest if your first swipe doesn't dislodge it. I figure a wasp in flight winds up to about 900,000 r.p.m.

When and if the nest falls, few of them will ride it to the ground. They'll swarm nearby looking for someone to murder. And within a few minutes they are great ones for saying, "Well, that's that!" and proceeding to build another nest. Then you may safely return and pick up all the bait one man will need in a day, all in a handy container.

More often we boys sought our bait in the woods, hunting nests attached to low-hanging tree limbs, to bushes or brier clumps. For this kind of "knocking wasp nests"—to give the sport its proper name—we first hied ourselves to the pine thickets. Here each man broke off the tip of a pine sapling, bushy and heavy with green needles, about two feet long. (I say "man" because we were preparing for man's work.) Trimming a handle at the thicker end of this pine top, we quickly had a weapon that could be effectively wielded in the manner of a tennis racket or table-tennis paddle. Your reflexes, I believe, will guide your use of this weapon.

Now you are ready to dig bait in the air. Lacking a barn between you and the enemy—a barn being the minimum waspproof protection—you must depend on alert caution. We sent one of our band ahead, chosen not for bravery but because it was his turn. He would try to knock down the nest, using his piney broom if it would reach or the fishing pole if necessary. His mission was only to dislodge the nest.

Then, propelled by the survival instinct, he'd fall back to our common line of defense.

The waspies shoot after the invaders. We whirl our pine tops furiously, backhanding, forehanding, fanning, swatting, swinging and praying. Anyone within a mile of the battlefield who isn't stone deaf can score each and every clean miss. A wasp-smitten boy howls like a wounded wolf. The language of the wasp robbers is elementary; it consists of one-word instructions muttered to the man who first gingerly approaches the nest, and who is not listening at all; then it becomes a busy, dead silence but for the swish of the pine needles—shattered by those blood-chilling squalls.

Some of us attained the status of two-brush men. A pine top in each hand is not a bad idea, providing you don't swish when you should have swoshed. To err is to learn that there is no room to run, or not enough, even with half of Georgia at your disposal.

The beginner is almost sure to get stung at least once in his first few raids. Nothing else will teach him the supreme caution needed. Nature lovers tell us that only the females and the workers have stingers, but any wasp is a "he" to me, because the wasp is so thoroughly virile. To the beginner I would say: Don't dally with this question. If you see a wasp zipping your way, you may safely assume it has a stinger. If your curiosity extends beyond that I can offer only sympathy.

I feel sure that only a couple of trifling matters keep the wasp from taking over the world now, without waiting to inherit. One is the apparent absence of mother love for her tiny grubs; there seems to be only a communal instinct to protect the nest, and when it hits the ground they either cannot find it or won't bother to lug it back up the tree. A question of strength here? Twaddle. I'm willing to bet that a wasp, certainly a redtail, could sling a jackrabbit over his shoulder and fly along home if he cared anything about jackrabbits.

It's a good thing, too, that grieving she-wasps don't spend days and weeks circling around, mad about their lost little grubs. Otherwise the fish-bait forays we made would have rendered a vast acreage of Georgia uninhabitable to humans.

Another wasp handicap is a sort of myopia about things on or very near the ground, proved by the fact that some wasps never find their own fallen nest—or else don't care a hoot about it. One summer an old graybeard of our town told us that everyone ought to know that wasps wear their eyes on top of their heads. "They can't see nothing below their line of flight," this character swore, "so if you drop flat on the ground after you knock the nest, why the waspies can't see you. They'll fly right on over and calm down after a while and you can pick up the nest without all this fuss you been makin.'"

He was a liar and I can prove it by the case of Hutt Pitts. A sad case of devotion to scientific research, Hutt was a martyr to folklore.

Hutt Pitts was a gangling, freckled kid of 13 or so years who was afflicted by spells of serious thinking. He said the old man's theory was logical and he was going to try it. Walt Stinson and I kept our doubts, both being normal lads who never had a real serious thought until we got through high school. We had located a big nest ripe for robbing in a patch of mixed bulrushes and briers down in Bussey's pasture, a rolling expanse of at least 10 acres. Thither we did go, Walt and I detouring via a pine thicket to arm ourselves as usual with pine-top bludgeons. Hutt went boldly on, armed with nothing but his new intelligence.

I drew the assignment to open the war, and duly knocked the nest out on the open grass. They boiled out to reconnoiter and I made it back to my pals before the wasps got a line on us. Walt and I set pine tops to churning the air with a great exuberance. Hutt flopped to the ground, face down.

They were redtails, and by the malice of those Walt and I were brushing away, I would judge they'd been banished from all other wasp communities as being unfit to live with. Along came a redtail that had been born deformed and wore his eyes underneath. Or perhaps, like the bumblebee that never heard an aeronautical engineer prove a bumblebee cannot fly, he simply didn't take any stock in the talk. Anyway, the most exposed part of Hutt was that point where his thin cotton breeches were the tightest. And the redtail peeled off into a power dive straight for Hutt's landing field. In one operation the wasp sat down on the spot Hutt usually sat and slipped poor, defenseless Hutt the hypo.

Hutt had only his good voice and long legs. He used both. He quit his theory and cleared Bussey's pasture in one of the fastest two-legged takeoffs I've ever witnessed. From a prone start he cleared the top rail of that old worm fence, on his third great bound, showing plenty of daylight. We saw no more of Hutt that day.

There was a country church over in that direction, holding an afternoon prayer meeting. In town later I just kept my mouth shut when old

Mr. Bussey was telling that, from what he heard, somebody over there got religion in a big way.

Well, wasps will do that.

Any man you meet who spent even part of his childhood in rural areas can tell you hair-raising tales about fighting wasps, but most that I've heard had the sole aim of knocking down the nest, with rocks, sticks, slingshots, air rifles, a .22 or a .410 bore shotgun. Few knew the value of the nest and contents. I was born on a plantation in Marion County, Georgia, and we moved when I was three to Columbus, Ga., which is not very rural. But I had cousins and assorted kinfolk strung all over Harris, Talbot and Marion counties. Families were close and we visited a lot; an entire summer wasn't too long a visit.

For all I know, the pine-top method of obtaining wasp nests was invented around Columbus by the Lucas boys, who were older chums of my big brother. We copied and perfected it, if perfection can be said to exist in this sport. I recall that one afternoon a group of us robbed 40 nests, we small fry having been charged with getting bait for four or five families bent on a joint fishing picnic. While I don't remember any count made of the catch, I know that at least 10 people had good strings of various panfish and an estimate of 100 total catch would be most conservative.

I was somewhere between 10 and 12 years old when wasps helped me complete a day of fishing that I've never been able to match in 40-odd years of trying since. My mother had taken me for the season to the big summer hotel at Warm Springs, which was a popular resort for many Columbus families before Roosevelt found it. (I don't mean that F.D.R. spoiled it, by any means, but that its fame was only local in my youth.) There was a traveling salesman at the hotel and he was sparking a grass widow who was also taking the waters. When the salesman said he would furnish the rig if I'd take them fishing, I jumped at the chance. I knew of a wonderful millpond, known as Parkman's Pond, about four miles from the hotel.

Borrowing two or three nests from the wasps, I also peeled the bark off a few pine cordwood sticks from the hotel kitchen's woodpile, catching a couple dozen flatheads under it. A worm about an inch long and tough-bodied, the flathead—sometimes called "sawyer"—is also an excellent bait and one that, by its toughness, overcomes the only drawback wasp grubs have as bait. Both appear about the same to a fish, but the wasp larva is a tender, fragile thing, inclined to slip the hook and easily stolen by smaller fish. I wanted to give this high-talking salesman a good run for his money.

Upon arrival at the pond, which lay on Pine Mountain in a beautiful, secluded woods setting, he and the grass widow disappeared. It dawned on me years later that this salesman did not have the great fishing yen I did. I went ahead and crushed the wasp nests I'd brought and baited up a likely spot in the pond, then used the flatheads for my hook. By the time the salesman and widow reappeared to lunch on the sandwiches put up for us at the hotel, I had caught 18 large bream. He gave me the munificent sum of 50¢ for my catch, obviously to take it back to the hotel with them and prove they had spent the day fishing.

After lunch, I went after more fish at another spot and the couple disappeared again. Fifty cents was a lot of money to me, and the arrangement suited me fine. It began to look like a promising career, I thought, when I hit a small school of bream and hauled in 10 of them in just a few moments. Didn't have time to string them, they bit so fast, each about three quarters of a pound.

Then I needed more wasp grubs for baiting up another spot and went hunting.

I got my nest, but in my haste a boiling-mad redtail got through to me. And I must admit another drawback in this connection: one slap from a redtail will cause anyone, man, beast or boy, to lose all interest in fishing—if not living. The couple turned up again at the pond when I sirened my distress and gave him my string, intending to quit fishing forever.

He gave me a quarter this time, which helped some, and I meandered down to the old mill, had some conversation with the miller, caught and ate handfuls of fresh, warm cornmeal as it ran slowly from the grinding rock and thus gradually regained a rosier view of the world in general. So much that I noticed a large school of bream had collected just below the millrace, under the swing of the wheel where the falling water had scooped out a pool. The fish were attracted by dribblings of meal escaping from the old grinding rocks.

My interest in fishing popped back to normal. I had to look no farther than the eaves of the mill itself for a large wasp nest, and robbing it was a fairly safe operation. Putting a hook to work with grubs, in about 30 minutes I had a third nice string of a dozen or more.

I found the salesman and his lady friend just getting ready to return to the hotel. He nodded with approval over my third catch and produced another 25¢. Thus we returned to the hotel, each carrying a heavy string of fish as proof of the afternoon's work. Looking back across the years, remembering the comely looks of the grass widow, the jaunty air and generosity of the salesman, I believe that I may say it was a highly satisfactory day for all concerned.

Once near Waverly Hall, in Harris County—also the scene of Pitts's last stand unarmed against the redtails—Henry Stinson, his son Walt and I used a wasp nest the size of a dinner plate and two others nearly as large to catch more than 60 mixed bream, blue cats and warmouth perch of quite respectable size. Henry Stinson was my mother's first cousin and the old Stinson home lay in Talbot County between two creeks known as Big Lazzer and Little Lazzer, producers of fine eating fish. On this expedition we used the burn-'em-out method on the wasps, which is simply a burning ball of crumpled paper attached to the end of a fishing pole and held under the nest. The flames, heat, and smoke either drive away or kill all the grown wasps, leaving the nest open for plucking. It is admittedly a cowardly attack and frowned upon by all wasp-knocking sportsmen. I recommend it.

The cowardly method helps solve the problem of wasp grubs being so slippery and soft on the hook. With untreated grubs, small fish that can't even mouth a hook steal them as fast as you can rebait and drop them in. If you'll just give the nest a light toasting, with care against burning it, the grubs will be hardened enough to stay on the hook, and apparently without changing the taste to a fish or altering the grub's attractive white color. The same result, of course, can be had by toasting the nest over a small fire of sticks or leaves, or even by leaving it briefly in a hot oven. No, I can't advise on what to tell your wife if she finds it there.

Flatheads or sawyers—if you think that toasted bait is carrying things too far—may be found between the bark and trunk on fallen pine trees. In using any of this grub bait, I find it best to use a small hook, either No. 8 or 10. And thread the grub carefully on a long-shank hook, rather than the short-shank style. A fish of any consequence is likely to take the whole grub and hookpoint in one grab.

If very small, bait-robbing fish are around in quantity, outwit them with all the foregoing tricks in combination, including the bribery of baiting up the fishing hole with a wasp's home or two to give the little beggars their fill. Then you can do business with the bigger fish.

After a hole is thoroughly smelled up with the fragrance of freshly crushed wasp grubs, you'll get action from fish worth your time.

The burn-out method is also effective with hornet nests. Don't question its humanity. I am prepared to argue that even poison gas would be justifiable against the horrible hornet. Only last summer my son-in-law came up with something new. There was a hornet's nest too near his house for comfort, for they have two small sons. He likes to fish, too. He got himself a small bottle of chloroform, waited until the hornets retired at dusk and stopped up that entrance hole at the nest's bottom with a chloroform-soaked rag. It worked. And the grubs seemed just a bit tougher than wasp grubs.

Hornet grubs would be tougher, naturally. A hornet deserves anything you can make happen to him. I rate him, ounce for ounce, the meanest thing alive. This merely bug-size bug, his whole body not half filling the bowl of a teaspoon except as to length, can vaccinate you with a quart and a pint of pure poison.

Point 2 of the indictment is that he is sneaky. He will throw himself in a curve at you, contrary to the straight-line flying done by most true wasps.

Even with a bat as large as the pine tops we used, whacking the hornet is like trying to hit a big-league pitcher with a fast ball and inside curve combined. Expect to get beaned every time.

Let me tell you about Joe Langdon and I am through with hornets. (Not that I ever had much to do with them anyway.) Joe came from the city ignorant of country life, hiring out as bookkeeper one summer at the packing shed of a big middle-Georgia peach orchard where I was putting in a few weeks' work for spending money. Joe had a fair reputation as a baseball pitcher in amateur and semi-pro circuits. He had control in baseball. What hurt him was wildness of curiosity. One day I showed him a hornet nest, about 50 feet from the shed on a low limb of a persimmon tree. It was a big one, populated by able-bodied hornets buzzing in and out the nest a dozen per minute. Joe had never seen anything like this, and he was fascinated, especially after I warned him that he could take greater liberties with a keg of dynamite than this innocent-looking bag of bugs.

The warning was effective for about three days, but every spare minute you'd see Joe intently watching that nest, learning about nature. Finally, temptation broke him. I saw him select a smooth, egg-sized stone off the ground, take his windup and fire it home. It struck the nest amidships, almost shattering it, and hornets—madder than hornets—boiled out in a cloud. Joe surveyed the results of his pitch smugly. But briefly. He wasn't more than 10 feet from the shed and could have stepped out of sight but maybe he thought a hornet wouldn't bother him at 40 feet. He must have seen it coming though, for he turned and made one quick step toward the shed. Then I heard the thud, like a hollow-point .22 bullet striking a soft pine board. Joe went down. Two of us toted him, nearly unconscious, to the office for first aid. On the back of his neck was a knot as big as my fist.

a crew of redtail wasps helped me train a good hound, convincing her she had no future as a squirrel dog. I want it understood that it was accidental on my part. I wouldn't sick a redtail on even a mad dog.

Queenie came of a pointer father and a hound-dog mother. From the first she inherited the keen nose of a bird dog; from her ma the endurance, speed and clear, bell-like voice of a good hound. She was the best rabbit dog I ever saw. Queenie knew she was good on rabbits and had no inferiority complexes: you might say she was an exuberant dog.

The trouble was that she, like some humans we all know, thought she was qualified as tops for any game, and she was always trying. Alas, how wrong. The very qualities that made her death on cotton-tails left her highly unfitted as a squirrel dog, especially for stillhunt-ing. She would drive every squirrel in the county, it seemed, to cover for good. But I couldn't get that through her head.

One late September day I planned a stillhunt in nearby woods well filled with hickory and oak, leaving Queenie carefully shut in the kitchen. But she had seen me with the shotgun. Somehow she got out after I was gone—probably someone let her out to stop the rack-et. It was just a breeze for her to pick up my scent and trail me to the carefully chosen hiding place in the woods where I lurked for the unwary squirrel. And when she bounded onto the scene, the still-hunt was over. This dog never knew the meaning of still, not for a second. So I began to scout in the big trees aimlessly.

We saw not even the bushy tail of a squirrel, thanks to this baying, bounding bitch. All I found was a redtail nest, and it was a whopper, about like a flattened basketball. I wanted it for a trophy, to keep a while and possibly use the grubs later for bait. And I wanted it intact, still attached to the limb if possible.

Mind you, revenge on the dog never entered my thoughts. That came as a bonus.

The redtails had built on a limb an inch in diameter growing straight out from the smooth bole of an old hickory. Due to our late-coming frosts in Georgia, the devils hadn't gone into hibernation yet. My aim was to sever the limb between the nest and the tree with a close-range shotgun blast. The pellets would be choked into a tight wad for some distance after leaving the barrel. With luck, I could creep close enough to clip that limb and still escape before the wasps riddled me.

So I creeped and fired, and my luck, plucky thing, stayed right with me. The nest, after my shot, hung by only a thin strip of bark on the underside of the limb. This strip peeled slowly and the nest came on down.

Queenie ran to meet it; joyously and loudly. Obviously she thought I had crippled some new brand of squirrel she ought to retrieve before he escaped. Redtails swarmed in her direction and I, with a shudder, stepped to shelter behind a handy oak tree. I didn't want to see this, and I didn't need to. Queenie's eloquent voice told the story.

I peeked once, to see if the first agonized howl had left her dead or alive. Definitely alive. It marked the first of many phenomenal leaps, this one a good 20 feet, toward home. Her lovely voice hit a strange new note, telling all of Harris County and part of adjoining Talbot that wasps were unfair! She also sang of pain, of shock and frustration—a symphony of woe from a hound flying low. Never had she shown speed anything like this in pursuit of a rabbit; could she have duplicated it on a Miami dog track I'd have wrecked the sport of greyhounds. And with every new flaming arrow that pierced her hide, Queenie told the world about it—all the suffering, the agony, the surprised hurt of those unjustly treated since the dawn of time.

Queenie never went squirrel hunting with me again, never wanted to. In fact, she gave me the shifty eye and wouldn't go anywhere with me and a gun unless I made it clear and plain I was destined for rabbit country. Head for the wasp-infested woods and she headed for home.

I'm still an ardent fisherman and I still use wasp nests when they're available. But looking back 40-odd years, sitting here with an old wasp wound twitching spasmodically when I think hard on it, it seems to me only fair that I should allow small boys and other daredevils to earn a bit of small change by bringing me my nests. I don't want to hog *any* sport.

taLL BuT SHORt

No, I never seen no flyin' saucers savin' the ones me wife used to throw at me. Lord rest her, she was a wonderful hand with the china— she could zero a cup on the back of me head at a hundred yards. But I have seen some wonderful things in the sky.

There's one phee-nomenon I'll tell ye about because I had a hand in it meself. 'Twas 60 years ago, when I was fresh in the Middle West from the old sod, and living off the land with me muzzle-loadin' shotgun.

Well, this day I was walkin' back from town, where I'd gone to buy some carpet tacks and a box of matches. The day was sunny but all of a suddint it clouded up, and I said to meself, "Heeney, me boy, we're in for a shower." But 'twasn't that at all. The skies were just black with passenger pigeons— so many of them they darkened the sun.

Down swooped a great flock of them and they lit on the branch of an oak. I had me shotgun along but when I searched me pockets, divil a bit of ammunition could I find. I felt the tacks, though, and they gave me an idea. First, I broke the heads off the matches and dropped 'em down the barrel. Then I rammed home a handful of tacks.

When I'd sneaked up to about 25 yards' range I took careful aim and touched 'er off. Not a single bird dropped—but neither did any of 'em fly away. "Hell's chimes!" I said. "What's this?" I walked over to the tree. And what did I find but every single pigeon with his feet tacked neatly to the tree. I'd shot a mite low.

"Well, I'll have ye anyway," I said, and hurried home to fetch an ax. When I got back I lit into that oak and soon had it chopped nearly all the way through. And just when I hit it the last lick, one of the pigeons let out a hoot, like a signal, and every bird started flappin' its wings.

And off they flew, takin' the tree with them.

Art Dyer

"and if i do marry you, will you subdue that fanatic passion of yours for fishing?"

"having a hard time getting back into the swing of things, crumwell?"

"teLL you what, i'LL throw in that fine dog
if you buy a set of LightNing roðs!"

Lightning-Rod Dog

by Capt. W. M. Molesworth

SPIKE, THE BIG LIVER-AND-WHITE
pointer, stood his first covey of birds
for us, and Roy and I moved up.
"Now, we'll spread wide after we shoot
on the rise," Roy said. "I'll circle that
brush to the right, and you to the left.

And if we miss him for as much as five minutes, we'll get in the saddle and find him."

"I'm ready," I said.

"We'll show that lightning-rod salesman!" Roy said grimly.

Spike held tight and we walked on past him and flushed the birds. It was a good rise, quail that had never been shot at getting up in the open and flying straight away. We each downed two. Spike retrieved the birds, then moved on. Soon he circled a motte of brush and was out of sight. Roy and I hurried after him, one on each side.

The big question was: Would Spike be in front of that brush or would he be gone?

I was moving at a half trot when I reached the edge of the brush, passed around a tree, and could see the other side. Just then I heard Roy call, "Here he is, on point."

I was so pleased I chuckled to myself. Then I got to thinking of that lightning-rod salesman maybe camped down the road someplace, waiting for his dog, and I laughed out loud.

I hurried on and Roy and I shot on another rise—Spike had found a brand-new covey.

We called Spike the lightning-rod dog because of the way we happened to get hold of him. I guess that dog had more owners than any other bird dog that ever lived—and he had all those owners at the same time. There was a spell when Roy and I came mighty close to breaking a fine friendship over who owned the dog.

"Take him out and kill a bird over him, and he's your dog for life," the lightning-rod salesman had told me, and that's exactly what I did—only not when he said I should. So now I was chuckling, because I was thinking of that salesman waiting for his dog.

It was funny, all right. But not to Roy—he kept getting mad all over again.

Down in the south-Texas country where I lived then, way back in the early 1890s, not many ranchmen had bird dogs. We went in for hounds, and we used them in hunting bears and cats and coons and suchlike. On my ranch, which was on the east prong of the Nueces River, there weren't enough bobwhites to bother with—nothing but fool quail, which I didn't consider much in the way of game. I wouldn't have put a bird dog down among them. They'd drive him crazy, running and hopping up and popping back down, then running again.

But a 15-mile ride to the prairie, toward Uvalde, would get a man better cover and plenty of bobwhites. Not many ranchmen hunted them, though, especially with dogs. Some men went after them with nets. Two would get on horseback, take hold of the ends of a net about 50 feet long, then ride hell-for-leather across some grass-covered flat until they flushed a covey of birds. The quail would get trapped in the net and the riders would let it fall, then go back and get their birds.

That was one way to hunt quail. But not me—I had a bird dog, and a mighty fine one. I hadn't much figured on ever owning a bird dog, since I had hound dogs and got plenty of hunting on my own ranch, including turkeys, deer, bears and cats. I probably wouldn't have bought that one except for the lightning-rod salesman trying to trick me. He got my trading blood churning, so I set out to outsmart him.

Roy, who lived on a ranch about seven miles away, had told me about the lightning-rod salesman with a bird dog. "If I ever set my eyes on that man again," Roy said, "there's going to be plenty of trouble. And that bird dog—if I ever catch him with it, I'm taking it."

Well sir, when that salesman drove up in front of my ranch house and I looked out and saw that fine-looking liver-and-white pointer trotting along beside the hack, I knew right away it was the same salesman—the one who'd tricked Roy.

I got set for him.

He was a smooth talker. All you have to do is drive through that country today and start counting lightning rods and you'll see what I mean. He sold those iron bars with little weather vanes and tin roosters on some of them for enough money to stock a section of land with calves. I believe it was around $200 a man had to pay for enough of the rods to give him what the salesman called real protection. I figure the rods cost him maybe $20.

He'd get you so worked up about lightning you'd see it jumping out of a clear sky, then he'd convince you that you could get in a house and be safe with lightning shooting down those lightning rods every five minutes. He sold them.

Now and then he'd hit a tough customer—some ranchman who just wouldn't trade. That's when he'd drag the pointer into the deal.

I told him I didn't want any lightning rods and there wasn't any use trying to sell them to me. "I like lightning," I told him, "and if I didn't, I wouldn't want a lot of iron spikes on my house to bring it to me."

I don't know whether lightning rods are worth anything or not. Most people in those days thought they really gave a man protection. Then for a long time everybody thought different and made jokes about the country hicks who bought lightning rods. Now I read where it's back the other way and that lightning rods really do help. I guess it's like spinach or vitamins—they're good for one generation and bad for the next.

I do know I didn't buy any lightning rods from the salesman. Finally he said, "Tell you what, I'll throw in that fine bird dog if you buy a set. He's out of the finest stock in the country—smell a bird a mile, solid as a rock. Got style. A dog like that ought to have a home. It's a shame to make him wander all over the country without a home, and you look like the man who'd give him the kind of home he ought to have. Why, I'll bet you've got a fine English-made double-gun in your house. . . ."

He sort of had me there. He could tell by the way I talked I was from England, and I did have a good English-made double-gun. He was a shrewd one, all right.

I said, "How much you take for the dog?"

"Well now, I hadn't figured on selling him," he said. "It wouldn't seem exactly right to sell a dog like that."

"Then what the devil do you call it when you throw him in on a deal to sell lightning rods?" I asked.

We started mentioning figures. He mentioned $50 and I mentioned $10. We got together on $22. I bought Spike, the lightning-rod dog. He was my dog now, bill of sale and all.

"Now, if I was you," he said, "I'd keep him tied up for a day."

"You don't have to worry about that," I told him.

"Then if you'll just take him out the second day and let him find a covey of birds and shoot one for him, why he's your dog for life. He'll stick right with you. I never saw such a dog. The way he loves to hunt, you couldn't pull him away from the man who shoots birds over him. Just tie him up good for a day, then shoot a bird over him."

I had a hard time keeping from laughing while he was telling me all that. I didn't tie that dog—I chained him. And I chained him inside the house so he'd have to chew through a wall or pick a lock even if he broke the collar.

Roy had told me about that salesman—and that dog.

"He goes around the country throwing in the bird dog to clinch sales," Roy said. "He tells the sucker to tie the dog up for a day, then take him out and kill a bird over him the second day and the dog is his for life. The sucker does that—you know you can hardly wait to take a fine dog out and try him. You're like a kid with a toy. You want to see the dog work.

"Well, that infernal salesman is camping down the road maybe 12 or 15 miles, just waiting. And the minute the sucker takes that dog out hunting, the dog goes ranging out wide, hunting in fine style, and when he's out of sight he takes off. He circles back, picks up the trail of those old bay horses the salesman drives and follows the trail. Pretty soon he and the salesman are heading out of the country.

"The sucker usually don't have any idea what's going on until it's too late. Then the salesman throws the dog in on another sale."

"How do you know all that?" I asked.

"How do I know it!" Roy snorted. "I bought him. He's my dog. I bought a set of those doggone rods to get him. If I ever see that salesman again—"

about noon of the second day that I had Spike—still chained up—I thought I'd have some fun with the lightning-rod salesman. So I got on my horse and rode along his trail. There he was, camped beside a spring. He seemed surprised and a little worried when I rode up.

"How's the dog?" he asked.

"Fit as a fiddle," I said.

"You take him hunting this morning like I said?"

"Sure did. Killed a dozen birds over him. Say, that dog's got style. Makes me feel like I traded a little hard with you. That dog's worth money."

"That's right," the salesman said, and his lower jaw sort of sagged down a little.

"And you were dead right about him not wanting to leave me after I shot a bird over him," I went on.

"That so?" he mumbled.

"Well, guess I'll be riding on," I said. "Good luck to you—and thanks!"

The salesman just mumbled and sat scratching his head.

When I figured he was out of the country, I rode over to Roy's house and told him to come back with me—I had something I wanted to show him. When he walked into the house and saw that bird dog, he said, "Why, that's my dog."

"No, he's my dog," I said. "I bought him. Got a bill of sale right here in my pocket."

"But I've got a bill of sale for him, too," Roy said. "He's my dog."

"No sir, he's mine," I told him. "My bill of sale is newer than yours— that makes it better. That's the law, you know—like a will."

"Aw, fiddlesticks!" Roy said. "I never figured you'd do a thing like that to me."

"i got the very Latest biLL of saLe," i said, "and spike is mine."

"Oh no? How about that hound you traded me that would run home and hide when he smelled a bear, and—"

"And how about that wind-broke horse?" he asked.

We argued for a little more. "Why didn't you tell me that swindler was around?" asked Roy.

"Because I was afraid you'd do something you'd be sorry for later. You're pretty hot-tempered. Anyway," I went on, "I figure we'll always hunt the dog together. What difference does it make who feeds him?"

Roy said he still figured I'd done pretty shoddy by him, but he guessed we would have some good times hunting with the dog. We did, plenty of them. We'd put Spike in my spring wagon and hitch my fastest team to it and we'd ride down to the prairie and hunt.

But we didn't do any hunting at all for three weeks after that salesman had gone, and we rode way down the road and talked to people, to be dead sure he really had gone.

You take a really fine bird dog and put him in birdy cover like we had on that prairie then, and you see something that makes a man feel glad he's alive. That big pointer would race off at top speed, then ease down and freeze on a covey. He was solid as a rock—and what a nose, and what style! We'd shoot on the rise and he'd retrieve the birds, then off he'd go. And chances were he'd bang into a new covey while he was hunting the scattered birds. That's the way it was then.

We bagged many a quail over him.

And if he ever felt sad because he couldn't follow that lightning-rod salesman all over the face of creation, why I couldn't tell it, except that he did do something that seemed a little odd. Once in a while when he was hunting he'd seem to forget about it and stand looking way off, holding his head high in the air and sort of sniffing, like he was wondering which way to go. Then sometimes when he was around the house he'd trot out to the road and look down it and hold his head high and sniff.

I didn't pay much attention—but I should have.

The next year that lightning-rod salesman came driving by my place again. He was careful to go way around Roy's place.

spike trotted out in the road, raised his head and sniffed. he had that faraway look in his eye.

I always did believe afterward that Spike put on an act that day. He growled at the salesman, and he never did make the least show of knowing him or the old team of bay horses. He acted the way he should have acted—like he was my dog and we were good friends. That tickled me, and when the salesman was gone, I said to Spike, "He's just another stranger to you, isn't he, old boy?"

Spike wagged his tail, which was his way of telling me I was dead right. Then Spike trotted out in the road, raised his head and sniffed—and he had that faraway look in his eye. I called and he came on back to the house.

The next morning he was gone. I got on my fastest horse and headed down the road. I was going to fix a lightning-rod salesman so he wouldn't want to ever see another bird dog. That salesman was really getting out of the country in a hurry. It was long past noon when I overtook him.

I rode up beside him and said, "All right, fellow. I want my bird dog."

He pulled up his team and looked at me in surprise. "Why, I don't know what you're talking about," he said.

"I'm talking about that bird dog—"

I stopped then, because I saw there wasn't any place in the hack to hide a bird dog. He didn't have Spike, just like he said. I didn't know what to say. I said, "I thought—oh, forget it. I'm sorry."

"It's all right," he said. He seemed anxious to get moving again. It should have struck me at the time that he acted a little peculiar in not getting riled up when I accused him.

I rode back home, getting in long after dark. No Spike. I sat up most of the night, thinking maybe he'd come in, and wondering what might have happened to him. Maybe a snake had hit him and he was out somewhere in the hills, sick. Maybe he'd followed my hound dogs out the night before and a bear had killed him. Maybe. . . .

The next morning when I was saddling my horse, thinking I'd ride around my ranch just on the chance, why it hit me like a flash of lightning hitting one of those lightning rods. That salesman had tricked me. He'd tied that dog in some brush along the road. That's what he'd done. Then, when I left, he'd gone back and got the dog. The more I thought of it, the surer I was.

I got on my horse and headed out. I was going to follow that salesman a hundred miles if I had to. I'd fix him.

I met Roy on the road. He was riding toward my house, and he had a silly smirk on his face that I didn't like. "You got time to ride over to my house?" he asked. "I got something I want to show you."

"No, I've got a little job to do right now."

Then I looked carefully at him, and I began to figure out that smirk. "You talking about what I'm thinking about?" I asked.

"I don't know what you mean," he said, still smirking.

"I mean a bird dog named Spike—a lightning-rod dog."

"I'm not saying a thing," he told me. "I just want you to ride over to my house. Got something I want to show you."

"If you've got him, he's mine," I said.

Just as I'd figured, Roy had Spike—chained up inside the house.

"All right, a joke's a joke, but this has gone far enough," I said. "I want my dog back."

"Not so fast," Roy said. "That's my dog."

"And how do you figure that?"

"I figure it because I've got a brand-new bill of sale for him."

"I'm the one that's got a bill of sale for him," I said.

"Yes, but mine's newer, so that makes it better—just like a will. Remember you told me that?"

He had me. There wasn't a thing I could do.

"You ought to be glad I got him," Roy added. "He was sitting up in the seat beside that salesman, and they were getting out of the country as fast as that old team of nags would take them."

"What I can't figure out to save my life," I told Roy, "is why that dog sneaked off in the night and went back to that salesman after having a good home and plenty of hunting for a year. Why, Spike acted like he didn't know the man—growled at him."

"An old love is a mighty strong thing in a dog's life," Roy said. "He never forgets. And dogs are wanderers. He just couldn't watch those horses jog on down the road and leave him. Now, about that bill of sale. I've got it right here—"

"Aw, throw it away," I said in disgust. "How much did you pay for him?"

"Well, right down here after the part that reads 'for and in consideration of,' you'll find 'twenty-five cents.' That's to make it legal."

"You bought him for a quarter?"

"That's right."

"And I paid $22 for him. I was robbed."

"You was robbed!" Roy shouted. "I bought a set of lightning rods to get him. Talk about being robbed—"

We looked at each other then, and we both laughed.

We never saw the lightning-rod salesman again. We heard later he met a sad fate when lightning hit that hack full of iron rods. But maybe somebody just made up that story.

I know one thing, though—we saw plenty of bobwhites flush in front of Spike. He was a great dog—a lightning-rod dog.

❖ ❖ ❖ ❖ ❖ ❖ ❖ ❖ ❖ ❖ ❖ ❖ ❖ ❖

taLL
but
short

Mountain lions
ain't cowardly,
like YOU say
they are. They're smart-smartest
critters in the hull cat family. It ain't
man they're afeard of, it's his gun. They
know it's pure pizen, so they let man be.

Cain't figure such things out? How do you know? There ain't nothin'
smarter than a good trailin' dog, yet it takes half a dozen of 'em to run a
lion, and even then they don't catch him but half the time.

I know lions is smart. Last fall a couple of my steers wandered off, so I rode
trail on 'em, hopin' to find 'em before some big cat did. All day long I rode
the canyons and shelves up at the north end of my spread, but I never did
find the steers. Towards nightfall, on my way home, I got off my hoss and
started up a draw toward a spring I knowed about, intendin' to get a drink
for myself and one for the hoss.

And right spang in the middle of that draw I run into a mountain lion, face
to face. All I had with me was a canvas bucket, and he knew it. He hunkered
down, started twitchin' his tail and then—zingo!—he was in the air and
comin' at me.

But somehow he misjudged the distance and went right over my head. I
whirled around just in time to see him hunkerin' down again. Then he made
another leap—and went over my head again. Four, five times he done that.
Then he just looked at me for a moment, shook his head and went trottin'
away into a little side draw.

I hustled back to my horse and got my saddle gun, cause I wanted to see
what that lion was up to. I followed him into the little draw, quiet as I
could. And then, peepin' around a rock, I seen him.

He was practicin' shorter jumps.

R. M. Grace

"i'm so glad you could stay, eileen. fred said he was bringing his best friend with him."

"we could have caught more if we'd known how to get these off."

My Husband Killed a Moose
by Clara Galbraith Knoll

THE HUNTER GOES HOME WITH HIS GAME—
AND THERE THE STORY USUALLY FADES OUT.
BUT THAT ISN'T THE END, FOLKS; IT'S ONLY
THE BEGINNING.

EARLY IN OCTOBER, 1948, MY husband killed a moose in Canada. It was a big fellow—weighed about 1,000 pounds, the guide said. It took three men to load it onto three pack-horses. They unloaded it directly onto our pickup, and the next morning we started for home, anxious to get there before the meat could spoil.

Twenty-four hours later we were at home, having driven steadily except for about one hour of rest. We took the whole animal (plus a small deer that Jack, my moose-killing husband, had got before he killed the moose) to the butcher, who prepared it for the locker. Then we went home to bed to sleep all day. At least, that's what I thought. But I was wrong. Jack was too hungry for moose meat.

At his insistence I went to the butcher and practically stood over him while he sawed off three huge T-bone steaks—one for Jack, one for me and one for our 15-year-old daughter, Lorena. I cooked them at once.

"Boy, oh, boy!" Jack must have said it a dozen times. "This is the stuff! It sure beats deer meat. I wish I'd never got that deer. You never get tired of moose the way you do other game."

It was, we all agreed, the finest steak we had ever eaten.

"I think the butcher would like to get that head out of his way," I told Jack.

"Yeah, I guess so," he answered. "I wonder if everybody has seen it yet?"

We showed the head—with the horns still on—to a fellow a few miles up the river. He hinted openly that his lodge could use such a fine moose trophy.

"Let 'em have it," I urged Jack while we were alone. "I don't want that sad-eyed thing mourning above me all the time."

Reluctantly he left it.

Jack was invited to join the Moose Lodge.

We ate moose steak and roasts and stews daily—in fact, almost three times a day. I gave a few cuts away. "Don't you go giving all this good meat away, now," Jack cautioned. "It's too good to pass out to strangers." We had recently moved to Clarkston, Washington, and knew very few people. "If we manage right, we'll have enough meat to last till spring."

We had Jack's boss and his wife come for dinner.

"Can't tell it from first-quality beef" was the verdict. Jack beamed and told again just how he had killed the moose.

The hide was in two pieces, as the guide had split the animal down the back. We nailed them both to the walls of the garage, sprayed them with DDT and locked the doors.

"If you get time, that hide ought to be fleshed," Jack told me. "I'd do it myself, but I have to get to work." I'd go out there and scrape off a bit or two, holding my breath as long as I could, then rush for fresh air. After three or four days I could hardly stand to get inside the garage even when I held my breath. Naturally, the car did not get in either. Then I revolted. Jack had a day off from work and he finished the job.

After the two pieces of hide were dry, he took a hacksaw and sawed one piece to about the size of his sleeping bag. I made a cover for it, and for a long time it lay on the floor of the living room—to be sure it stayed flat, he said. After we had either hopped over it or walked around it for so long that none of us could walk straight over any floor, he slid it under Lorena's bed while she was away at school.

Lots of Resistance

The other side I wrapped with the deer hide. Jack told me exactly how to do it before he started for work. Gosh, that hide was stiff! I struggled with it, tugged and pushed it, hugged and squeezed it and finally sat on it till I got it tied up into two gunnysacks, one over each end and lapped in the middle, but not much. Jack measured the length and breadth to be sure it could go by parcel post, then took it to the post office. The hides were on their way to Wisconsin to be tanned and made into a jacket.

I don't like liver. Instead of taking the moose liver to the butcher, I cut it up myself—into eight big pieces, so my two cats would have a feast. They didn't like liver either—not moose liver anyway. I put the eight pieces in the locker.

By now we had two lockers. The meat wouldn't all fit in one. The butcher thought the moose weighed 1,200 pounds. The local paper said 1,600.

A couple of days after we had taken the head away, Jack came home late.

"Hey, help me unload this, will you?" he called.

"Unload what?" I asked. I should have known. He had brought

it was aLways a sHock to wake up witH tHose
HORNS HOVERiNG oveR me.

home the moose horns. The fellow up the river had weakened when
he heard how much it would cost to mount the trophy, and Jack had
salvaged the horns.

"Wait till I get the garage door opened," I called.

"What do you want to open the garage now for? Let's get these
horns out of here."

Again I should have known. We took them into the house. I couldn't
figure out what to do with them.

"We'll have to put them in our bedroom," Jack said. So we did. They
had a lot of some kind of salt on them, which spilled all over the
place. Jack cheerfully ordered me to put newspapers under them if I
didn't want the salt on the rugs. I put the newspapers down. The
horns were placed rather precariously on a chest of drawers and held
in position by wire. I never woke up and saw those horns hovering
over me without getting a feeling of surprise—not pleasant, either.

A Surprise for Lorena

One day the horns fell off. "I can't have those things up there any
longer," I insisted.

"Well, they'll have to go in Lorena's room, then," he said. She was away at school at the time. When she got home and found them taking up a big corner of the floor of her room, she didn't say anything for a minute.

"Well," she finally remarked, "I guess I'm the only girl in town with moose horns in her bedroom."

We had become accustomed to moose meat and had ceased to praise it at every meal. In fact, we ate it now without comment.

We were invited out to dinner.

"That beef was good, for a change, wasn't it?" Jack said when we got home. "I didn't realize there was so much difference."

I brought home a hunk of moose liver and cooked it. I could hardly stay in the kitchen. None of us could eat it. But the cats liked it fairly well after it was cooked.

One day late in February we had a roast that looked good and tasted good.

"Say, this is fine," Jack praised it with his mouth full. "Why don't you cook it this way all the time?"

"That's venison," I said.

It had been nearly two months since we had sent the hides away, and we had heard nothing about them. I wrote to the company and got a reply. They had not received the hides.

Jack really raved. How could the post office lose as big a package as that? I wondered too. But it was insured, and I did not feel too bad about the loss.

"What does he want those hides for?" the delivery man asked.

78

"Gosh," I said, "just collect your insurance and be glad to get some cash out of those hides instead of having to pay out for them."

He was horrified. "For a measly $25? That's all I insured them for," he mourned.

He had the post office begin the job of tracing. Eventually the hides were found. Where? Why, in the dead-parcel office in Seattle.

"A good place for them," was my first reaction. The postal people reported that the hides were spoiled, but Jack insisted on getting them back.

"Say," the delivery man asked when he brought them, *"just what does he want those hides for?"* I couldn't answer that one.

I held my nose and kept as far away as possible while Jack spread the hides out on the dining-room floor and inspected them. They were perfectly all right. Possibly a little stiffer, but still sort of curled together. So I wrestled with them again and sent them to a tanner in Oregon.

"It seems like that meat is awfully dry," Jack commented in April. "Why don't you cook it the way you did when we first got it?"

In May he asked, "Aren't your folks ever coming to visit us?" I was surprised, although he always welcomed my relatives. "They might like to eat some of that meat," he said.

About the first of June we took a two-week vacation. It was also a vacation from moose meat. When we got home, I cooked a big steak that looked delicious.

"It still tastes like moose," Jack said. "Isn't it near enough gone that we can have something else once in a while?"

I'd have been glad of a change too, but after all, he had killed the moose and it seemed foolish to pay out money for meat when we had two lockers of it.

"I'm afraid I'm getting a cancer," Jack said one day. "One of the symptoms is a lack of appetite for meat."

I bought some hamburger and we all relished it. He didn't mention the cancer again.

There was a notice from the post office about a C.O.D. package. I went down and paid nearly $20 to get the hides back. This time they were leather. After Jack had inspected them, I wrapped them again and put them in a trunk. They are still there.

On August 1 we moved to a new home. I knew, of course, that the horns and hide and leather must go with us, but the foot? (I forgot to mention before that Jack had also brought a front foot of the moose home from Canada. All these months it had been in the garage.) I saw him trying to sneak something on the loaded moving truck. Yes, it was the foot, and it still smelled.

"For heaven's sake!" I said when we unloaded at the new house. "We can't have that foot on the back porch."

He looked hurt. But after three or four days, when the flies had just about crowded us out, he sadly hung the foot up in a back shed. It's still there.

Lots of Meat Left

It was past the middle of August. "I'm going to see for myself how much meat is left in the lockers," Jack said.

He was quite discouraged by what he saw. "I didn't know the lockers were so big," he said.

One day, shortly after we moved, he called excitedly. "I've got an idea! Where's my brace and bit and a big bolt? I'll need you to help me."

I hurried in to hear about his big idea and soon found myself sitting on the horns while he worked hard at boring a hole through the part that held the two sides together. It all added up to a place to hang the horns— in the living room. They had been right in the middle of the floor ever since we moved, so I was glad to get them anywhere out of the way. Now they hang majestically above our heads and are mighty dusty.

Jack came home off the graveyard shift one morning and banged his lunch pail down hard. "It's bad enough to eat that meat at home all the time," he declared, *but not for lunch.*"

I practically snorted. "Well, you killed it, and we have to eat it before you can get another one."

"I don't think I want to get one every year," he said slowly. "I guess now I really know what that Canadian guide meant when he said, 'I hardly ever kill a moose anymore if I can help it.'"

The guide had said Jack's moose weighed 1,000 pounds. The butcher said 1,200, the newspaper said 1,600. Me? Well, I can look a preacher straight in the eye and say, "My husband killed a MOOSE. It weighed 1,800 pounds."

It was now almost a year since that big day when Jack got his first moose. He came home from the locker with an odd gleam in his eyes. "Say," he said, "I believe if we manage it right we'll have enough meat to last till spring."

"If we don't manage to get rid of it a little bit faster," I replied, "we'll have enough meat to last forever." And we just about did.

❖ ❖ ❖ ❖ ❖ ❖ ❖ ❖ ❖ ❖ ❖ ❖ ❖ ❖

fallout - Dr. Marion Smith thought he had seven quail when his dog Topper brought him three more than the four he shot. Then he discovered a hole in his game pocket through which the birds had been falling out for Topper to retrieve.
- Roy Trefftzs, STILLWATER (OK) DAILY NEWS-PRESS.

point of no return - Dick Jennings says Bob Meeks, Arkansas guide, was netting a seven-pound bass when the Texan who caught it brags, "Why, down in Texas we throw back itty-bitty ones like that." Said Meeks as he calmly tossed the lunker overboard, "That's funny, Mister, we do too."
- Wally Forste, CINCINNATI (OH) POST AND TIME STAR.

poetic justice - Wenatchee district game protectors are still chuckling over the thief who thought he was swiping the hindquarters of an elk, which was actually part of a mule carcass slated for coyote bait.
- Tom McAllister, PORTLAND (OR) OREGON JOURNAL.

mug shot - A Marquette, Michigan, archer was just lighting his pipe when a deer appeared. The bow hunter managed to get off one shot that not only sent the arrow and his pipe, but also his false teeth, sailing some 60 feet when the pipe stem became entangled with the bow string. - Tom McNally, CHICAGO (IL) TRIBUNE.

fall guy - Pity the West Springfield hunter who sighted a distant deer from his perch in a tree, fell out of the tree in his excitement, landed athwart a buck he hadn't even seen feeding underneath him and didn't get either of them.
- Buddy Marceau, SPRINGFIELD (MA) UNION.

❖ ❖ ❖ ❖ ❖ ❖ ❖ ❖ ❖ ❖ ❖ ❖ ❖ ❖

taLL
BuT
SHORt

Skinnin' a bear ain't much of a chore less'n the bear is alive. Then it's chancy. I mind the time my brother-in-law and me used to hunt black bears for their skins, cause a man could make himself a little eatin'-and-drinkin' money by sellin' good undamaged hides. Aim for the head so's not to cut up the fur, and then skin 'im out. That's the way we done.

I mind once we was up near that big canebrake across the river. All of a sudden a big black hops across the path and goes into the cane. I climb me a tree and I spots him in there—a plum easy shot. I aim, pull the trigger, an' down he goes. I git down out of the tree, put my big huntin' knife betwixt my teeth an' crawl into the cane. That bear, he never moves. But jest when I'm gonna stick him in the throat up he gits, madder'n the devil in church.

I aim to skin him out, and he aims to do the same for me. He's got more natural equipment for the job, so he wins the first 15 rounds. Soon I ain't got a stitch on me but my collar and a pair of shoes. But I git in a few licks now an' then with my knife.

But that brother-in-law of mine! He stands outside the cane an' screeches an' hollers. I wonder, "How come he's so worried about me? He owes me eight dollars this bear could save for him." But he screeches an' hollers an' carries on. After a while the bear turns around to see what this ruckus is all about an' I slip my knife into him where it does the most good. This time he dies permanent.

I turn around and yell to my brother-in-law, "Hey, whut's ailin' you, anyway? Why you doin' all that screechin'?"

"Why?" he says. "Man, the careless way you tackled that bear you sure was fixin' to spoil the hide!"

Charles L. Culley

"don't be afraid, children, it's only daddy!
a hunting trip always makes a new man of him!"

"must be two birds."

The Great Deception of '51

by Paul Quinnett

my parents were convinced that the path to enlightenment led to the schoolhouse door, but i was just as sure that it led to fisher's pond.

MY FATHER BOUGHT ME MY first rod and reel when I was 7 years old, and therefore (I have always argued), he was ultimately responsible for my great deception of '51. A lifelong fisherman himself, he should have known better than to fill the mind of an innocent child with visions of rising trout, battling bass, the attraction of an eddy in the morning sun and the grace of a rod arched against the struggle of an unseen fish. I felt a sense of shock and disbelief that when the great deception finally came to an end, my father should have been so angry.

By all accounts my youth was flecked with indiscretions. I generally preferred going to the dentist to going to school, and considered an education something to be acquired involuntarily. When it came to getting to and from the schoolhouse I was the kind of child who,

as Grandma used to say, "bears watching." If my parents rested from their vigilance I was as likely to end up at Fisher's Pond as in Mr. Funderberg's geometry class. I rarely profited from the painful consequences of my actions, and no amount of "talkin' to" could convince me that the path to enlightenment led to the library and not to the pond. And then, one day, I was released from the confines of elementary school.

Almost six feet tall, I had become an embarrassment to the faculty and was "advanced" to junior high school. Junior high meant riding a bicycle to and from the inquisition rather than taking the bus and, with the freedom inspired by a two-wheeler, I was drawn to Fisher's Pond like a sliver of iron to a five-pound magnet.

Fisher's Pond, when I think back on that sweet place, must have been designed and built for boys under 15. It was a two-acre lake teeming with bluegills, perch, catfish and a band of marauding large-mouth bass that, according to legend, had attacked and nearly drowned Ronnie Kahler's cocker spaniel.

The great deception of '51 lasted eight glorious days.

"How was your first day at school?" Mother asked as I came in the house.

"OK," I lied.

"Did you get the classes you wanted?"

"I got everything I wanted," I said, not quite lying.

"What's that mud doing on your shoes?"

"Soccer. We had to play soccer."

"You *did* go to school?"

I looked my mother square in the eye (I learned early to look straight at people when telling whoppers). "Where else would I go?" I straightforwardly replied.

For the next seven days I intended to go to school. But on that first morning I had hooked and lost a gigantic bass sometime during first-period algebra (this fish essentially ended my career as an atomic scientist), and no matter how I fought the handlebars, the bicycle was magically deflected away from the junior high school and drawn up the road to Fisher's Pond. My bike was a thing possessed.

I learned to catch and release gamefish during those halcyon days because bringing them home would have been tantamount to suicide. Each afternoon, when the fishing slowed, I stashed my gear in a culvert and started home while working up a new batch of lies.

I knew that once apprehended, I would be grounded to my bedroom through the rest of puberty. As the days passed, my estimates of detention stretched from weeks to months. On the fifth day I figured I would be locked in my room until age 35 without my collection of outdoor magazines.

At two o'clock on the sixth day I had decided to give up and confess, muster up some crocodile tears and throw myself on the mercy of my parents. The guilt was overwhelming. Just then the bass that had nearly swallowed Ronnie Kahler (or was it his dog?) started dragging my bobber across the pond. My remorse dissolved in a spray of water and a parted line.

But my delinquency could not last forever, and the hour of reckoning came two days later.

My mother stood with her hands on her hips, lips pursed in a stern line. "I never thought I would live to see the day a son of mine would be a sneak," she said. She put arms around me and, expecting to be flogged, I struggled in her warm hug. Then she began to cry. It was worse than a thousand whippings.

I started crying too. I had not counted on this peculiar business of mother-love. Somewhere she had gotten the notion that I was a troubled youth and that I'd cut school because I was psychologically underdeveloped, frightened by the responsibility of young adulthood or too immature to face new teachers. She was worried about me. "No boy," she later explained to Father, "would skip school to go fishing just because he wanted to go fishing. He must be afraid of something."

That I was running the greatest scam of my life never occurred to her. I was afraid, however, that her enlightened analysis of my psyche might be lost on Father.

Later that evening I made a vow to take up schooling seriously. I made this decision for two reasons. Neither had to do with the fact that I was barely literate and had difficulty making change of a dollar in a family where education was prized second only to baptism.

The first reason was one of conscience. I could no longer concoct stories to conceal my addiction to fishing from the woman who loved me—although years later I managed to overcome this troublesome scruple.

The second reason, if less honorable, was every bit as compelling. My father, a one-time professional boxer and a man unencumbered by the finesse of proper child psychology, asked me out on the back porch.

"Your mother says you cut school to go fishing." He sat looking out over the strawberry patch that stretched down the half acre to our fence.

"I couldn't help it," I said. "Besides, they were really biting. You said you had to get them while the getting was good."

Father looked at me as if I was a pup who had pointed a grasshopper. "I want to explain this so you understand it," he said.

"Sure, Dad." I was relieved he hadn't handed me a pair of eight-ounce gloves.

"Do you see that milkweed sticking up out of the strawberries about 30 yards down the patch?"

I could see it, so I nodded.

"Well," he said, "I promised your mother I would never lay a hand on you. But back in college I was a tremendous dropkicker and that milkweed is just about where you'll land if you skip school to go fishing again."

taLL
But
short

Didn't get your buck, did you, son? Well, you ain't going to get one, either. And since I've took a liking to you I'm going to tell you why. It's just that you've lived in the city too long, and you gotta learn country ways if you hope to get a buck.

'Course the Indians did their stalking all rigged out in some critter's hide, making out they meant no harm a-tall; but that's going a mite too far.

Trouble is, when you get up in the morning you wash yourself all over with smelly soap. When you get through shaving you rub your face with gook out of a bottle. You can't comb your hair without you put some stickum on it.

Why, son, when you get to the woods and take your stand, any deer without asthma can wind you for a mile. But then you make it wuss—you light a cigarette.

Now, like I said, you gotta learn country ways. Us boys here, we allus hang our clothes in the woodshed, so they'll smell like wood. And we keep our boots in the sheep stable so they'll smell like sheep.

And then, on the morning we hunt, we eat fried mush and drink cider for breakfast, because deer like corn and apples. Of course the deer can wind us for quite a piece and it smells to them like an old goat or sheep is eating corn and apples, so they come in to investigate—and that's where we get our meat.

Only time we ever come back empty-handed was one day last season. Dog-gone if Lem Hawkins's collie dog don't wind a bunch of us starting out. He rounds us up and keeps us with Lem's flock of sheep all day. And we'd have spent the night in Lem's sheep stable too, only I shot my old thutty-thutty through the roof and Lem comes out to see what the trouble is and calls off the dog.

Dennis B. Roth

"mind if i ask you a question?"

"how many times must i tell you—never aim at the whole flock."

The Lion and the Lamb
by Percy Brown

EL BARREGO WAS OBVIOUSLY A NUT; NO SANE MAN WOULD TRAIL A COUGAR BY MOONLIGHT! HERE'S THE ROLLICKING TALE OF ONE WHO DID JUST THAT—WITH ASTONISHING RESULTS.

He smiled proudly. "I have bes' dogs for Leon. And I'm bes' hunter for Leon!"

*A*LTHOUGH THE SOUND WAS little more than a low, guttural sigh, it jerked Al and me awake like a pistol shot.

I sat up in my bunk. "What in the world's that?" I asked uneasily.

My rancher friend rolled up in his blankets and covered his head. "Oh it's just the frisky colts playin' around in the corral—I hope," he muttered in a sleep-drugged voice.

The corral and water lot were behind the house, less than 100 yards up the canyon, and the mares and their young frequently came in at night to drink. Figuring that Al was right, I plopped back on the bunk and shut my eyes. However, sleep didn't come easily; I kept remembering that sudden, eerie sound.

After a short, restless nap, I awakened at dawn. Al was propped up in bed, smoking a cigarette, as he does each morning before arising.

"Let's go out and scout around a bit," I suggested. "Maybe we can find out what made that queer sound last night."

"OK," agreed Al. "That's just what I was figurin' on doing—the more I think about it, the more that noise gets under my skin."

He picked up his rifle and we went out to the pole corral, but saw nothing amiss. We started to return to the house, but on second thought I decided to investigate the stunted oaks that fringed the ranch opening. I walked up a deep-rutted trail, watching the ground for tracks—and almost stepped into a small pool of black, crusted blood!

One glance at the open, bare ground nearby told me what had happened. Within a dozen feet of the oaks, a huge mountain lion had stalked a colt, pounced on it and struck it down like a bolt of lightning. The noise we'd heard was the death gasp of the dying animal!

"Al!" I called. "Come here, quick!"

The rancher came on the run, saw the unmistakable evidence and said, "Let's follow him!"

Job for a Lion Hunter

The lion had dragged the heavy colt back into the oaks, so Al hoisted his rifle to ready and followed the blood-splattered trail. About 50 yards from where the colt had been brought down we found its carcass. The lion had eaten his fill, raked a few leaves and twigs over the remains and gone on his way.

Al shook his head gloomily. "That's the first killer lion that's been in this part of New Mexico in years. We better hurry and hunt him down—he'll likely eat every colt I've got before he quits!" His face suddenly brightened. "Say, I just remembered! The state lion hunter is over at Slim Jones's place—I'll jump in the pickup and go get him."

Slim's place was 86 miles away, but with luck Al could get the hunter's dogs back in time to take up the renegade's trail.

"Hop to it," I said. "I'll keep a sharp watch and shoot the rascal if he comes back to eat another meal."

I doubted that the lion would be back. Apparently the critter was a large old tom—and lions grow big and old only because they use their brains. He'd probably strike down another colt when hunger again gnawed at his middle.

Al should have made the round trip for the lion hunter in a matter of hours, but he did not get back until after dark. Luck had been against him; the man had packed into a wilderness area and wouldn't be back for a week or more.

"I may have done some good, though," said the rancher. "I passed the word around that I'd pay $300 for the killer lion's scalp—maybe that'll attract a hunter or two."

And it did. A couple of days later, a Mexican came jogging up to the ranch on a bony horse, followed by four ribby hounds. When we went out to greet him, the fellow inquired about the reward.

"Yes," admitted Al, "I'll pay 300 good American dollars for that killer lion's carcass!"

"Bien," smiled the berry-brown one. "Me, I'm catch 'im for you, I'm for sure!"

The newcomer informed us he worked at a nearby sheep ranch, but would return in a day or two to catch the lion. He gave his name as Antonio Carlos Chavez. "But people, they call me El Barrego!" he said, decidedly pleased with the odd name.

"El Barrego" is Spanish for "the Lamb." Mexicans use the term to decribe an easygoing, simple fellow. Since most whom I know would resent the label, I thought perhaps I'd misunderstood him. "El Barrego?" I inquired.

"Sí, señor! An' the bes' leon hunter that ever come from Mejico!"

Well, I could see that the Lamb, despite his odd name, suffered from no inhibitions.

Neither Al nor I took the fellow seriously, so when we returned from riding the next day, we were surprised to find him sprawled out in the shade of the barn, enjoying a late-afternoon siesta. When we opened the clanking gate, he sat up and rubbed his eyes. "I'm already prepare' to hunt," he announced, as if getting ready for a lion hunt had been an exhausting task.

"OK," said Al. "Turn your horse and pack animal into the feedlot and let 'em eat."

The bony horse and the gaunt mule were led to their dinner, and then Al spotted the four hounds. "I'll go into the pantry and get some meat for them," he said.

El Barrego held up his hand. "No, señor, gracias! We hunt soon an' dogs do better little hongry—"

"You're going to hunt soon?" broke in Al. "Why, it'll be night before you can get started good!"

"Sí! I'm hunt in night—mebbe all night!"

This was too much for Al; he shook his head. "Beats anything I ever heard of! Why, you'll ride off a bluff—break your neck!"

I was as astonished as Al. I've known some mighty good lion hunters, old Ben Lilly included, but not one of them ever made a habit of running lions after dark. The Mexican was an unusual lion hunter, indeed—or a nut!

I could see that Al doubted the man's sanity. He invited the fellow in to eat supper with us, but he kept a wary eye on him.

By the time we'd finished eating, the sun had set. El Barrego went out, saddled his horse and rode from the ranch, his lanky pack of dogs following obediently. Just before disappearing from sight, he turned in the saddle, pointed toward the almost-full moon and called, "I'm mebbe hunt all night—got lotsa light!"

"Good luck!" returned Al and I—and we meant it. Any man who would ride these rough mountains by the light of the moon certainly would need luck to return alive!

However, the Lamb did return alive with the rising sun. And, as his nag jogged into the corral, Al and I were astonished to see how fresh the hunter, his horse and his dogs all appeared.

"You hunt all night?" Al pressed, a bit suspiciously.

"Sí, señor—but no luck!"

Al didn't comment, but I saw him rub his chin thoughtfully.

After taking care of his horse and dogs, El Barrego partook of a hearty breakfast, then pushed his chair back and began chatting about hunting, ranch life—everything but sleep. Finally I dropped a pointed hint. "There's a bedroll in the back room if you want to sleep. You've probably had a hard night."

"No so hard," shrugged the Mexican.

Al and I finally saddled our horses and left to do the day's riding. When we returned that evening, we learned that the hunter had not used the bedroll. "I'm take fine siesta," he admitted when we asked him if he'd had his rest. "An' now I'm go hunt some more."

Again, promptly at sunrise, El Barrego returned to the ranch as fresh as the proverbial daisy. Al shook his head. "You sure don't look like you've hunted all night!" he challenged.

"Sure, I'm hunt all the night," insisted the Mexican. "But, again she's no luck—mebbe pretty soon I'm catch 'im!"

As we rode that day, Al and I talked of little else but the unusual hunter. And Al, who is usually the soul of trustfulness, was as suspicious as a breath-smelling wife. "His dogs and his horse come back fresher'n when they leave," he complained. "We better follow him tonight and see what's cooking. There's a joker in the woodpile—and I aim to find it!"

When we reached the ranch that evening, El Barrego was truly refreshed, he admitted, and ready to tackle another night's hunt. After a hearty supper, he boarded his nag and headed for the wilderness, his dogs following in the horse's tracks. At a discreet distance, two other horsemen brought up the rear. But the Mexican didn't know that curiosity had got the better of Al and me.

The horse's tracks were easily followed in the soft light of dusk. Even when they left the trail and skirted a long, broken drop-off, we followed like true-trailing bloodhounds.

Just as dusk gave way to a brilliant moonlit night, we heard a cry directly ahead and reined our horses up sharply. Seconds ticked by, then—"Ba-a-a! Ba-a-a!"

"A sheep!" blurted Al.

"A lamb!" I corrected.

"What the—how'd a lamb get way over here? The nearest sheep ranch is 20 miles away!"

"Maybe El Barrego is imitating his namesake—a lamb!"

Al slapped the pommel. "That's it! By golly, we're going to learn something tonight, I do believe!"

And we did. Plenty.

We stayed on the hunter's tracks, but we kept our ears tuned to the blatting. When we neared the source of the cry, we left our horses and pussy-footed forward. Al, who was in the lead, suddenly jerked up short and pointed toward a wide-spreading tree. A horse—El Barrego's horse—was tied to a low-hanging limb. Then, as we strained our eyes, we saw the Mexican. He was bending over, unrolling something. Presently the fellow lay down with a contented sigh.

"Hell's bells!" whispered Al. "He's got a pallet—he's fixin' to sleep here!"

He broke off and headed angrily toward the Mexican, as if he intended to truly put the man to sleep, with a haymaker. However, as we approached, a dog gave a low growl and El Barrego raised himself to an elbow. Then he saw us and got to his feet. "Señores!" he exclaimed happily. "You come hunt with me!" He waved toward the clean mat of pine needles. "Lie down here; mebbe soon we have the good hunt."

"Hunt, hell!" exploded Al. "Looks like a slumber party to me!"

"At Las' He Come!"

Just then a dog gave a low growl and the hunter put a finger to his lips: "Sh-h-h!" he whispered. "At las' he come, I'm think!"

Al and I saw the four gaunt hounds tied to a nearby bush, their hackles raised, looking off into the night. They were facing into the wind, and the Mexican called our attention to that fact. "Sí, señores, we got the big luck! He is come!"

"Who's come?" challenged Al suspiciously.

"Him—the big leon!" The Mexican untied his mount. "We get on horses, we run the leon, quick!"

Al and I raced back and boarded our ponies. El Barrego released the dogs—and the chase was on! The ribby hounds barged into the moonlit night, baying furiously. A hundred yards they ran, then 200. The wild clamor seemed to increase in intensity by the second. "Bien!" exclaimed the Mexican. "We have the fast leon run, no?"

"Are you sure they're running a lion?" I asked.

"Sí, señor! Am I not train 'em from little pups?"

"They're sure burning the breeze!" exclaimed Al. "It *must* be a lion to run like that!"

The Mexican smiled proudly. "I have the bes' dogs for leon. An' me, I'm the bes' hunter for leon!"

"Maybe we better hurry and try to follow 'em," said Al. "They might go out of hearing distance pretty soon!"

"I no think so," returned the hunter. "I pick this place for hunt so we hear dogs many miles. Anyway, they catch 'im before one mile, maybe—two mile for sure!"

Even before he'd finished, the hounds burst loose with their happy treed cry. "They got 'im!" whooped Al. "Let's hurry and get over there!"

He reined his horse toward the yowling dogs, but the Mexican cut in ahead of him. "I'm lead the way, señor," he announced. "Me, I'm never ride off the bluff."

It is perhaps just as well that the hunter took the lead; Al or I might have blundered into loose slides or other dangerous going. The Mexican's gangling mount jogged along at a fast, even gait; apparently he was an old hand at this sort of thing.

Finally we came near the frantic hounds. El Barrego snapped on his flashlight, then ran the pencil beam up a tall, bushy pine. It finally came to rest on a large, tan-brown object. "El leon!" exclaimed the Mexican, handing me the flashlight and bringing his ancient .30/30 to his shoulder. The lion was looking the other way, and we couldn't see his head. But there was no need to. From his huge size, we knew he was the killer.

"Shoot him," called Al. "And the $300 is yours."

The gun blared—and the great, tawny cat came plummeting to the earth in a shower of broken limbs and twigs. The gaunt hounds pounced upon it and began worrying its lifeless body.

The hunter tied the huge lion across his saddle, took hold of the reins and started back the way we'd come. The house was in the opposite direction, and Al called, "Let's go straight to the ranch!"

El Barrego shook his head. "No, we must go back for the little one!"

Almost as mystified as before, we plodded back toward the wide-branched tree, rounded a jutting ridge and again heard a lamb's plaintive cries filling the woods! El Barrego headed straight toward the blatting, passing the big tree and continuing on toward a dead, gaunt juniper. The cries came so thick now it seemed a dozen sheep were corraled there. The Mexican snapped on his flashlight, sent the beam up and brought it to a stop on a small wooden cage. "Here, little one," he called. "We are return! An' your job, she is done!"

Al's voice was shaky as he demanded, "Now, El Barrego, tell me the meaning of all this!"

El Barrego smiled. "Is all very simple! I tie little barrego—a lamb—high in tree. He is safe, sí? But lonely! He cry, for mother. Leon hear cry. Then he come for to get meal. But me, I'm wait. My dogs too. Soon they smell leon—they give the growl, push up the hair on backs. I turn loose the dogs. The race, she is always short!" He shrugged heavily. "For this, I'm called El Barrego. Sí?"

"Yes," gulped Al, "I see—I see a lot of things, now. It cost me $300 for this lesson, but it's worth it!"

I agreed heartily, for it hadn't cost me a cent.

taLL
BUT
SHORt

Alf was put out at Les, and I don't blame him. A crowd of us was swapping yarns. Alf told about a city feller he was guiding, and how all the city feller got was black gnat bites while using what Alf calls "highfalutin flies" whilst he, Alf, soon caught the limit using (unbeknown to the city feller) stick grubs for bait.

Then Les spoke up. "See this silver dollar? Has the year of my birth on it so I carry it as a lucky piece."

"So's you can figure out how old you be, you mean!" sniffs Alf.

Side talk didn't stop Les. He went right on. "Nearly lost this dollar fishing up on Loon Pond."

"Now don't say you used it for bait," Alf put in.

"No," Les replied, "but another time I'd be tempted to, way things turned out. Somehow the dollar fell out of my pocket. I heard it splash, saw it go down—and so help me, a black bass made off with it."

"Sure," commented Alf, "you caught the bass and found your dollar in his belly."

"No," says Les, "the cuss had spent the dollar afore I landed him. In his belly I found a cob pipe, package of fine cut and 78 cents in change."

"Oh, so!" howled Alf. "Such being the case, how do you account for you now having the silver dollar?"

"Let me finish," Les hollers back. "Just afore sundown I was skittering among the lily pads when lucky for me I hooked the fish that had sold the pipe and tobacco. He had my dollar tucked in his gill."

Alf gave Les a hard look and left without saying goodbye. He's a good guide, too.

Ellis Gurney Thayer

98

"Hey mister!"

"Father, here, is the salesman.
I'm just the decoy."

Mekong Madness

by Charles W. Stockwell

i hunted willingly, though i knew i'd die of heat or become an hors d'oeuvre for one of the local carnivore.

the tiger stood by uncertainly as i loaded my shotgun, tore open the door and fell down the steps into a thorn bush.

*A*LONG THE GREAT MEKONG River, which rises in Tibet and forms the border between Thailand and Laos, are many dense, lush jungles. There are tigers, elephants, boars, bison (gaur), deer and quite a few Communist bandits in the area. I'm an Army officer, and while I was stationed in Laos during 1961 and 1962, I often hunted with my Lao and Thai friends, mostly for tigers, though we were impartial about what went into the bag.

The average inhabitant of this area likes to go night hunting with a muzzle-loading gun, a weak head lamp and a faith in the religion of his fathers that would move mountains. The fact that his weapon is ineffective against half the jungle denizens he encounters doesn't worry him. He usually goes barefooted (because it is quieter) and prefers you to do the same. After hunting all night, he drinks several cups of coffee resembling crankcase oil in color and consistency, and he is off to spend the day shooting green parrots and jungle fowl in the 120° heat that bakes the jungle.

It was to this regimen that I willingly committed my soul, knowing full well that I would probably die of heat exhaustion or become an hors d'oeuvre for one of the local carnivore. My reason, which seemed sound at the time, was to get a shot at one of those tigers that live on barking deer and village dogs. I accomplished my objective, but not exactly as I had planned.

The natives, another officer and I usually took a dugout canoe from Vientiane and ventured 10 or 15 miles upriver. Distance meant nothing, actually, since the biggest tiger around lived on the north edge of the airport in Vientiane. But it isn't playing the game to shoot your trophy within city limits.

There were a few game trails and logging roads that ran perpendicular to the Mekong. We would trudge along one of these until our strength and perspiration ran out. On the way, we would shoot a few

my friend was disturbed to find he was sharing bathroom
facilities with a migrant Leopard.

birds or monkeys for our evening meal. Monkey meat was high on
the menu, and a specific of half monkey blood and half Scotch
whisky was considered to be the aperitif par excellence, though for
the life of me I could not appreciate why.

All along the trail we would find great, nasty-looking pugmarks
firmly impressed in the soft dust. I was also impressed. At last we
would reach the camping spot beside some small, greenish pool,
which was, I didn't doubt, at least 50 percent ammonia since it was
the only water hole around. There we would prepare our evening
meal, using the glutinous rice that had been cooked before we left,
rolled in a banana leaf and carried in the sash of one of our companions. These sashes are most handy. Besides serving as belt and carrying case, they are useful as a towel, headdress, dishcloth and bathing
suit. It all depends on what you need them for.

One rather horrid experience occurred once while we were eating
dinner. Our guns were all unloaded and stacked away, and the old
sticky rice was going the rounds when we heard a rustle in the bushes. As everyone looked, a big tiger strolled through the underbrush
about 50 feet away. Obviously, he was heading for the water hole.
And, strangely, he never paid the slightest mind to any one of us.
Since our guns were between him and us, I don't exaggerate when I
say there was a moment of confusion in our camp. Another time, one
of the group wandered down in the early morning to a similar water

hole to brush his teeth and found to his surprise that a leopard had come to share the facilities.

I guess it is the snakes, more than any other thing, that made the most vivid impression on me. Don't let anyone tell you there aren't a lot of snakes in that kind of country. My boss's house back in Vientiane had a garden that produced more snakes than flowers. One even came to a cocktail party he was giving and grabbed a parakeet (or was it a lovebird?) out of its cage. But that's another story. The time my goosebumps had goosebumps was one night when I was out hunting alone except for a small boy who had been detailed to report when and if the Communist guerrillas grabbed me. I was barefooted, as custom decreed, and had a dim flashlight taped to the barrel of my gun. When a noise sounded quite close, I tried to pick up the source with my light. Thinking that it was probably a wild boar, I took another step or two. Then it sounded again, this time at my feet. When my light struck the snake, which was coiled in some leaves not two feet away, I could see that it was a banded krait. My young companion and I had some difficulty getting started, but when we did he led me by 10 feet all the way back to camp.

My fearless friends would sometimes go hunting with me, and a favorite trick was to wade barefooted up or down the tiny streams in the dark since the streams were better to hunt than the trails. My friends always fired before I did, probably because I was more interested in what was close to me than in the game standing on the edge of the jungle. Even in the daytime, you weren't safe. Once a small bamboo snake crawled up my pant leg when I was sitting on the ground. Nijinsky, the fabulous Russian ballet dancer, could never have equalled the leap I took from a sitting start. Another time, when crawling through some bushes, I bumped into the man ahead. As I looked up, he shot the head off a king cobra that was so close he almost touched it with his gun.

I never could quite get the hang of night hunting. There was the time I had fired both barrels and was desperately trying to reload my old Czechoslovakian shotgun, shucking 12-gauge shells out of my vest like corn off a cob. Two enormous wild boars raced around me like Indians attacking a wagon train, due to my weak-minded and ill-directed assault. They kept brandishing those long, sharp snickersnees appended to their jaws. And all the while I was attempting to keep my lamp on them.

for variation, we would shoot cane rats at night in the bamboo thickets, using crossbows, which are still a major jungle weapon. Or I would use the homemade muzzleloader my Thai friends presented to me. It fired homemade powder and bits of lead, iron or gravel. This was wadded down with shreds of coconut husks and fired with a primer made of caps from a child's cap gun. These light, long-barreled guns were excellent for birds, but if you ran into anything larger than a barking deer, it was obligatory to back quietly to the nearest tree and climb rapidly, thorns or no. The boars and gaur seemed to know you were relatively defenseless and stood their ground. Even barking deer would turn on the dogs and, with their long fangs, inflict nasty-looking bites on our curs.

Well, let me get to my tiger shoot. One weekend, I teamed up with a friendly Thai policeman who liked to hunt. The Thais are among the most cordial and hospitable people in the world. We had in mind a certain tiger with a penchant for canine cuisine, having eaten several village dogs.

We tethered a nondescript dog about 25 feet in front of some tall slabs of rock that stuck up from the crest of a wooded ridge. We then crept back into the bushes and lay down on an anthill that up to now had gone unnoticed. The dog, having seen our marksmanship demonstrated earlier on small game, had no faith in our ability to protect him when and if a tiger appeared. Dusk slowly came to the jungle.

I never actually heard the tiger come, but the dog became agitated and began doing Immelmanns on the end of his leash. Then I became aware of something breathing heavily on the other side of the rock against which I rested. It wasn't me, since I had been holding my breath for several minutes. Apparently, the tiger didn't like something about the setup. Maybe he was too conscious of our proximity (about 12 feet from him, according to the pugmarks we found the next day). At any rate, the tiger departed and shortly thereafter the policeman, the dog and I—in that order—did likewise.

Later, when I passed that way again, I spent the night in a valley near that same ridge. We had bedded down at night in a native hut built, as usual, on stilts and constructed of thatch and grass. We stripped down to our shorts and soon fell asleep. Suddenly the dog gave a yowl and jumped straight up into the air. A tiger was snuffling outside our door in a horribly suggestive way. Or maybe it was me snuffling, but anyhow the tiger was there.

I grabbed my double-barreled shotgun and hastily loaded it. Then, clad only in a shooting light, I tore open the door and fell down the steps into the middle of a thorn bush. The tiger was standing uncertainly on the other side of the clearing. I let him have both barrels. Then, slamming a couple of more shells in the gun, I cut an armload of limbs off the bushes through which he had dived.

Later, when we built a bonfire that looked like the second burning of Rome, we carefully searched the ground for blood. I knew I had hit him! With all that buckshot I couldn't have missed. Then I picked up one of the empty shell cases. I had grabbed the wrong shells in the dark and had shot the tiger with No. 7½ birdshot.

Whether it is true or not, I was told later that they killed the tiger, a young male, the next day almost a mile away. The man who shot him stated with a straight face that he didn't know whether to skin the tiger or melt him down for the lead. The tiger's rear had been full of birdshot.

That is the reason I don't have a tiger skin in the den amid all my other dust collectors from Africa, Canada, Europe and Russia. But, you know, I enjoyed my hunting in the Land of a Thousand Parasols just as much.

❖ ❖ ❖ ❖ ❖ ❖ ❖ ❖ ❖ ❖ ❖ ❖

taLL But SHORT

"What I don't like about mules," said Yancey, "is that they got no imagination."

"No imagination!" scoffed old Gilhooley. "Why, I druv mule teams in the Army for 26 years, and they could think up more ways of annoying me than the Katzenjammer Kids."

"That's instinct," said Yancey. "They do those things without thinking."

"Bah!" said old Gilhooley. "Mules have more imagination than you have. Why, take that team my pa had on his farm out on the prairie. Raised corn, my pa did. And every night, after dark, he'd hitch up his mules and drive a wagonload of it to town."

"Drove at night, did he? Musta stole those mules."

"No such a thing. A man couldn't drive on that prairie during the day. Got so all-fired hot it would fry your brains. One night, though, pa got to fooling around with the jug a little too long. He fell asleep and didn't wake till dawn. But the wagon was all loaded, so he figured he'd hustle to town anyway."

"What's all this got to do with a mule's imagination?" asked Yancey.

"Wait'll I tell you. In a coupla hours the sun was blazing down like the business end of a blowtorch. But pa kept right on going. All of a sudden he hears a noise behind him like a thousand rifles going off. "Injuns!' he says, and jumps off the wagon. But it wa'nt Injuns. By golly, that sun was so hot it was popping the corn! The white stuff just poured outa that wagon and rolled across the prairie.

"Well sir, those mules turned around, took one look at it and laid down. They figured it was snow and just naturally froze to death!"

Roy E. Crary

"what's the matter, Herbert? cat got your tongue?"

"not having much luck, are we?"

Edgy Rider
by Patrick F. McManus

AS A CHILD I CONSTANTLY begged my father to buy me a pony. One day I extracted from him the promise that if he saw an inexpensive steed at the auction he would buy it for me. He came home with a pig.

"Where's my pony?" I demanded.

He pointed to the pig. "You're lookin' at it."

I named the pig Trigger.

Naturally, I was enraged. Other farm kids had their own ponies to gallop about on while I had to ride a stupid pig! On the pig's behalf, I'll say that he cared as much for being ridden as I did for riding him.

"Whoa, Trigger!" I'd scream at the pig.

"*Oink oink squeeeeeeeeeee!*" he'd reply, and race along a barbwire fence in an attempt to saw me into four equal sections.

The great humiliation, though, was when my pony-owning friends would come over to play cowboys. The only one who sat short in the saddle, I always had to be the villain. "Hey, Podner," one of the guys would say to his sidekick, "I think ol' Black Bart is trying to sneak up on us—I just heard his horse oink!" Then they'd laugh.

That fall I had little trouble containing my grief when Trigger was transformed into hams and salt pork. Seldom does one have the opportunity of eating an adversary without being subjected to criticism. Nevertheless, I was still without a suitable steed.

Crazy Eddie Muldoon, who lived on a nearby farm and was also horseless, came up with the theory that cows might be employed as satisfactory mounts. The theory seemed reasonable enough to me, as any wild scheme did in those days, and I agreed to help him test it.

"Since it's my idea, I'll do the hard part," explained Crazy Eddie. "That means you get to ride the cow first and have all the fun."

This seemed uncharacteristically generous of him, and I inquired as to the exact nature of the "hard part." He said it consisted of study-ing the results of the experiment and thinking up ways by which the

ride might be improved upon. "And I have to keep a watch out for Pa, too," he concluded. "He's down working in the bottom pasture right now. But we don't want him showing up while you're riding the cow. Understand?"

I understood. Mr. Muldoon was a burly Irishman with a volcanic temper, and he strongly objected to scientific experiments being conducted on his livestock.

Getting on board a cow turned out to be more difficult than either of us had supposed. Crazy Eddie would try to boost me up, but the cow would give us an indignant look and walk away, with me clawing at her hide and Eddie running along grunting and gasping and trying to shove me topside. Finally, he said he had another idea, which was that I would climb up on a shed roof overhanging the barnyard and, when he drove a cow past, I would drop down on her back.

"And presto!" he exclaimed obscurely.

As soon as I was perched on the edge of the roof, Crazy Eddie cut out from the herd a huge Holstein, one approximately the size of a Sherman tank, and drove her unsuspectingly beneath my perch. According to plan, I dropped down on the cow's broad back, grabbing her bell collar as I landed. And presto! The Holstein emitted a terrified bellow, leaped straight up in the air and executed a rolling figure eight with full twist. That was for openers, a little warmup exercise to get out the kinks and limber up her muscles. Then she stretched out like a greyhound after a mechanical rabbit and did four three-second laps around the barnyard, a maneuver apparently intended to build momentum for a straight shot down the narrow lane behind the barn.

With hands locked like sweating visegrips around the bell collar, and every toe gripping cowhide, I stuck to the back of the Holstein like a hungry, 65-pound bobcat, which may have been exactly what the cow thought I was. During the first moments of my ride, I wondered vaguely if Mr. Muldoon's cows were equipped with burglar alarms, for there was a terrible din in my ears; only later did I attribute this fierce clanging to the cowbell.

About midway down the lane, I managed to unlatch my eyelids—a mistake, as I instantly realized, for the first thing I saw was a compounding of my troubles. There, plodding up the lane toward us, possibly with nothing more on his mind than the question of what his wife had fixed for lunch, was Mr. Muldoon. Now, unknown to me, the barnyard antics of the Holstein had terrorized the rest of the herd, which was stampeding along immediately behind us. It was this wild and violent spectacle that greeted Mr. Muldoon as he glanced up from his preoccupation with picking his way through patches of cow spoor laid down with the singular indiscrimination for which cows are noted. In retrospect, this preoccupation bore a certain similarity to concern about a few drops of rain just before one falls in a lake.

Overcoming the momentary paralysis that accompanied his first sight of us, Mr. Muldoon exploded into furious activity, which consisted largely of jumping up and down and waving his arms. The clanging of the burglar-alarm cowbell prevented me from hearing what he was shouting, which was probably just as well. Perceiving that his efforts to flag down the herd were not only ineffective but, if anything, were increasing the cows' r.p.m., Mr. Muldoon turned and began to sprint ahead of us at a rate that under normal circumstances I'm sure I would have marveled at. As it was, we passed over him as if he were a tansy weed rooted in the ground.

My dismount from the Holstein was facilitated by a low-hanging limb on a tree at the end of the lane. I bounced several times, finally coming to rest in a posture similar to that associated with a lump of mush. Fortunately, I had landed beyond the exit of the lane, and the herd of cows that thundered close behind showed the good sportsmanship of fanning out on both sides of me. Mr. Muldoon had not been so lucky. When he came hobbling up to see if I was still alive, I noted that he appeared to have been pressed in a giant waffle iron, and one none too clean at that. I choked out the story of the experiment to him, and he showed considerable interest in it, mentioning in passing that he could scarcely wait to debrief Eddie in the woodshed. Crazy Eddie, I might add, was at that very moment in the house busting open his piggy bank to see if he had enough money for a bus ticket to another state. I was happy to learn that he came up short by several dollars.

Ny craving for a suitable mount, by which I mean one that did not go *oink* or *moo,* was never to be satisfied.

Years later, my own children began begging me for a horse. At the time, we lived in one of the humbler sections of suburbia, an area that, through some oversight of the planning commission, remained zoned for agriculture. This meant that it was legally possible for us to keep a horse on our two acres. I decided to broach the subject to my wife.

"I've been thinking," I broached, "every kid should have a horse. Caring for a horse gives a kid a sense of responsibility."

"What do you need a horse for?" Bun replied. "You already have a four-wheel-drive pickup with racing stripes and a chrome rollbar."

That woman can be incredibly dense at times. "Not for me! Ha! I can just see myself, dressed up like Clint Eastwood in *High Plains Drifter*, galloping off into the sunset!" Actually, I didn't look bad that way, not bad at all, but I wasn't about to give Bun the satisfaction of think-ing she'd had one of her suspicions confirmed. "Yes, by gosh, I think we should buy the kids a horse."

"But we don't even have a barn!" Bun wailed.

"We can turn the garage into a barn," I explained. "Listen, all we need is a little imagination."

"All you need is a good psychiatrist," she muttered. Later, when I was copping a plea of temporary insanity, I would remind her of that mutter.

Contrary to popular opinion, it is remarkably easy to buy a horse, but only if you know absolutely nothing about horses. I found an ad in the classified section of the newspaper that stated: "Good kids' horse, $150." It seemed like a steal. Surely, I thought, at this very moment hordes of eager horse buyers are converging upon the fool-ish soul who is offering such a fantastic bargain. I dialed the number, and the man who answered—he spoke in the soft, country drawl I had expected—confirmed that indeed he was all but overrun with potential buyers.

"I don't want to sell Pokey to just anyone, though," he told me. "Since you sound like a man who knows horses, I'd be happy to bring him by your place so you can take a look at him."

I said I'd be delighted if he would do that and gave him the address of my spread. Scarcely had I hung up the phone than an old pickup truck with a horse in the back came rattling down my driveway.

A lanky cowboy emerged from the cab of the pickup. Extending a hard-callused hand, he said, "Name's Bill. You the man what's lookin' for a good kids' horse?"

I replied that I was indeed that person. By this time, my brood of moppets were bouncing up and down around me, clapping their lit-tle hands together and screaming, "Buy him! Buy him!"

"Hush," I scolded them. "I'm going to have to have a closer look at him first."

"Sure thing," Bill said. He dropped the tailgate of the pickup and ordered the horse, "Step out of there, Pokey." Amazingly, the horse backed up and stepped down out of the pickup. Then the cowboy scooped up our little three-year-old and set her on Pokey's back. I'll swear that horse turned and smiled affectionately at Erin. He walked ever so carefully around the yard, stopping every time she teetered one way or the other until the little girl recovered her balance, and then he'd plod on.

My wife, who was witnessing the performance, also seemed impressed with the horse's gentleness, or so I judged from the fact that she had ceased pounding her chest in an apparent effort to get her heart started again.

"What'd I tell you," Bill said. "Pokey's a great kids' horse."

There was no doubt about it. While Bill was lifting Erin back down, I was writing out the check. Perhaps I wouldn't have been so hasty if I'd had the good sense to study the horse's face more carefully. When I finally did so, I had the distinct impression that it bore a combination of features that reminded me of W. C. Fields and, in a different mood, of Richard Widmark in one of his roles as a homicidal maniac. Probably just my imagination, though, I said to myself.

One little incident before Bill departed also caused me some wonder about my purchase. As Bill was wringing my hand as though I had just saved his life, Pokey plodded softly up behind him. I assumed the horse was going to give his former master an affectionate goodbye nudge. Instead, he clamped half a dozen yellow teeth onto the cowboy's shoulder. I recall the smirking look in the horse's eyes as Bill danced about, silently mouthing curses as he reached back and twisted one of Pokey's ears until the animal unlocked its jaws. Bill grinned sheepishly, if you can imagine the grin of a sheep that has just been gnawed on by a coyote. "A little game Pokey and I play," he said.

"Really?" I said. "I would have guessed that hurt like heck."

Bill casually flicked a tear off his cheek. "Naw! Heck no. Well, be seein' you."

Contrary to his last remark, I never saw Bill again. But I can say in all honesty, I really would have liked to, and preferably in some remote area where his shouts for help would have been to no avail.

Within a month, I could not look at Pokey without seeing "glue factory" written all over him. The only thing that saved him from taking up residence on the back side of postage stamps was that the children loved him. And, as far as I could determine, he loved the children. He lived with us for 10 years, providing the children with almost as much pleasure as he did the tack-shop owner, the feedstore proprietor, the farrier and the veterinarian. I viewed him largely as a malevolent machine for transforming five-dollar bills into fertilizer for my garden.

I must admit that I had some ulterior motives in acquiring a horse. My wife's charges that I intended to satisfy the cowboy fantasies of my childhood were, of course, too ridiculous to dignify even with denial. I did think, however, that the horse might come in handy for elk hunting, so I went out and purchased some of the essential gear for that purpose.

Bun knows nothing about elk hunting, but even so I thought her response to my acquisitions was uncouth, to say the least. Personally, I find it unladylike for a woman to stagger about holding her sides while squealing hysterically.

"Laugh all you want," I told her, "but if you weren't so ignorant of the subject you'd know that nine out of 10 elk hunters wear cowboy hats. Cowboy boots are the only safe footwear for stirrups—anybody knows that. And the brush on the sides of trails will tear your legs to pieces if you don't have a good pair of chaps. The leather vest—well, you'd just be surprised at how handy a leather vest is when you're hunting elk!"

"B-but the spurs!" she gasped. "The sp-spurs!"

I didn't even try to explain the spurs. I mean, if a woman is so ignorant of elk hunting that she doesn't know about spurs, there's no point in trying to educate her.

It had been 20 years and more since I had ridden a horse, or a pig or cow for that matter, so before embarking on Pokey myself I considered it only prudent to study the horse's style while the children rode him about the two acres I now referred to in taverns as the "back 40." With the older children, he would gallop at a moderate gait around the fenced pasture, slowing for the corners and in general taking every precaution not to unseat the young riders. Several knowledgeable horse persons who observed him thus in action told me I couldn't have found a better kids' horse. I would nod knowingly, chewing on a grass straw as I pushed my cowboy hat back with my thumb.

One day when the kids were off at school, I told Bun, "I think I'll take a little ride on Pokey, just to shape him up for elk season."

"I was wondering why you had your chaps on," she said. "Where are your—*hee! hee!*—spurs?"

"The spurs are for later," I said, ignoring her mirthful outburst. "Now, come on out to the back 40 with me. I may need some assistance."

"Okay," she agreed, "but if you think I'm going elk hunting with you to help you get on and off your horse, you're crazy."

Perhaps it was fate that dictated I would have to suffer insults in my pursuit of horsemanship. The problem was, I had not yet been willing to mortgage the house in order to swing financing for a saddle. Since the children mounted the horse by using the board fence as a ladder, I figured I could do the same. This procedure, however, was made easier if someone held the horse's bridle while the mounting was taking place.

Maybe my imagination was acting up, but the expression on Pokey's face that day seemed more Richard Widmark than W. C. Fields. Nevertheless, I climbed the fence and, while Bun maneuvered the horse up close, I threw a leg over him. So far, so good. I took up the reins and told Bun to step back.

"Giddap," I said.

Nothing.

"Giddap!" I said, louder.

Still no response whatsoever. I looked at Bun. She shrugged her shoulders.

"GIDDAP, you miserable *bleep-of-a-bleep!*"

The *bleep-of-a-bleep* lowered his head, against which he had now flattened his ears, but refused to budge.

Once more I shouted "Giddap," but this time I dug my heels into his flanks. Before my hat hit the ground at the starting point, we were at the far end of the back 40. But it was not so simple as that.

The smooth, rhythmic lope with which Pokey carried the children about the pasture had been replaced by a gait closely simulating the motion of a jackhammer—a thousand-pound jackhammer. My eyeglasses flew off, the fillings in my teeth popped loose, my vertebrae rattled like castanets. With the instincts of a natural horseman, I hauled back on the reins. Unfortunately, the motion of the horse had bounced me so far forward, I had to stretch the reins far back behind me, and even then couldn't get the slack out of them. But this problem had ceased to concern me, since I now had another distraction.

For those unfamiliar with a horse's anatomy, there is a large bone at the point where the neck hooks on to the rest of him, technically speaking. I now found myself astraddle this bone, pounding against it at a rate of five times per second. On the scale of discomfort, this sensation rated somewhere between unbearable and unbelievable, thus motivating me to take defensive action. I flopped forward and wrapped both arms around the beast's neck, a move that had the purpose not only of enabling me to hold on but possibly to strangle the horse into submission. Alas, at that moment, Pokey cut sharply around a corner, so that I was swung beneath his neck. We arrived back at the starting point with me suspended from the horse's neck in the manner of a two-toed sloth from a limb. Pokey came to a reluctant halt, and I dropped to the ground. Calmly, I picked up my hat, beat the dust out of it on my chaps and strolled over to Bun, who was sagged against the fence doing her impression of a limp noodle.

"Want to see any more trick riding?" I asked.

Despite my air of nonchalance, the ride had taken its toll on me. Suddenly, in fact, I detected what I thought was the symptom of a heart attack—an excruciating pain in my shoulder. Then, collecting my wits, I reached back, got hold of an ear and twisted it until Pokey unclamped his jaws.

Pokey was truly a great kids' horse. But he hated adults.

Our next yard sale included a cowboy hat, cowboy boots, chaps and a leather vest.

"Don't you want to sell the spurs?" Bun asked.

"No, I'm keeping them," I said, "just in case I ever run into Bill again!"

❖ ❖ ❖ ❖ ❖ ❖ ❖ ❖ ❖ ❖ ❖ ❖ ❖

taLL
BuT SHORt

We were arguing in Pop Robertson's place about which animal is the smartest in the matter of self-preservation. And we were getting nowhere. "You settle it, Pop," someone spoke up.

Pop is always willing to do that. He runs a little country store, dispensing sagebrush philosophy along with canned goods, bottled cheer, and hunting information.

"No question in my mind about it," Pop said. "The coyote is the smartest critter on four feet. Why, I remember one time we were camping on the upper Sespe in winter. Game was scarce and even the coyotes were starving. Got so hunger drove 'em right into camp at night for scraps of food. But the little devils were real clever about it.

"One of 'em would come to the edge of camp and attract our attention, while the others sneaked around behind us and raided the grub sacks. This one would stand there in the darkness watching us. All we could see was his eyes, glowing in the flickering firelight. So we'd draw a bead between the eyes and shoot. But we never could find a dead coyote.

"That irked us. So one night I rigged up a rifle rest out of my bedroll, and got right between that big coyote's eyes as soon as he showed them. I knew he was big because the eyes were spaced so far apart. But just as I was squeezing the trigger a pine knot in the fire flared up, and in the bright light I saw two coyotes standing pretty close together and staring at me. But each coyote was staring with only one eye—the outside ones were closed.

"That's how them pesky devils had been fooling us. We'd been shooting right between 'em!"

Bill Brent

we hauled him back to camp on a flatcar and peeled off the widest black skin i ever saw.

And One Ketched Perry

by Charles Elliott

ALMOST ANYBODY WITH gumption who lives between Tatum Creek and Trader's Hill in Georgia will tell you that Perry Barbour was the greatest bear hunter in history. And they ought to know. There aren't many of those marsh-dwelling citizens who haven't slogged behind the swamper trying to corner a black in some remote pocket of the Okefenokee Swamp.

I once asked Perry how many bruins he'd killed over an active half century.

"I've ketched 300 of the shaggy varmints," he replied. "And one ketched me."

Perry inherited his dislike, distrust and disdain of the whole bear clan from his father, Obediah. The story that wore out the grapevines around the Okefenokee for two decades was how Obediah, armed with only a pine knot, killed a bear of uncommon size.

The elder Barbour was a giant of a man, six and a half feet tall, and one of the mightiest swampers of his day. He'd lost a lot of hogs to thieving blacks on the edge of the swamp, and he waged practically a lone battle against them. The feud came to a climax one night when he found a black rogue in his hog pen, feasting on the porker he'd fattened for his winter meat. Obediah was so mad he didn't even take time to get a gun. Vaulting into the pen, he jumped on the black, encircled its shaggy neck with a mighty arm and pulled the roaring animal off his pig. They tumbled through the pole fence, smashing it to toothpicks, before the bear twisted free of the headlock. Lunging at the elder Barbour, it tore his shirt off and slashed his skin deep enough to make the crimson spurt. But Obediah didn't give an inch. He stood toe to toe with the thieving black, trading blow for blow and bellow for bellow.

Finally, with a bawl of rage, the bear pulled away and streaked for the safety of the woods. The swamper snatched up a pine knot, sprinted after it and caught it near the edge of a thicket. The bear swung to face him and threw a punch that had broken the bristled neck of many a hog. They grappled and went down, clawing and beating each other. The man was the first to roll free. He got a new grip on the shaggy hide, held on and clubbed the animal to death with the pine knot.

So, it's no surprise that up until he was 50 years old, Obediah's son Perry spent most of his days making war on bruins in and around the Okefenokee. Rogue bears were his special quarry. They're the ones that have a cultivated taste for honey, hogs and the cattle that range the wild grasslands, which run the great morass. Seldom a week passed that some rogue-plagued neighbor didn't come looking to Perry for help. He never turned down a request to knock off a bear, and often he tackled the job all alone.

I came near to going with Perry on that hunt when the bear ketched him, however. I was there when a neighbor came to his house and told us about finding the carcass of his prize heifer that a bear had killed and dragged off into the swamp.

"The critters et a dozen of my hogs, I reckon," the neighbor complained. "I didn't mind dividin' pork with 'im, but that there heifer was worth her weight in minted money. And now I'm mad enough t' chew a plug outer the hind end of the next black devil I meet."

I'd arranged to meet a man in Waycross in a couple of hours, and it was only by severe self-discipline that I squelched an impulse to go with Perry. But I stayed on while he called his dogs and went in the house to get his gun.

I knew most of his dogs by name and voice: Jailor, Rock, Bull, Nellie and a couple of pups with whom I'd never been on the trail. Jailor was Perry's favorite, and mine too. I recall the first time I saw the Barbour dogs. I asked if they were a special breed, whelped and trained for running swamp bears.

"They're pure cur," Perry said. "I figured out the mixture myself, with hound, bulldog, collie and a few other kinds thrown in fer looks and size. From the hounds they git the nose. From the collie they git the brains. And the bulldog in 'em jest don't give a hoot whether they run day or night, or in the thickest part of the swamp."

I guess I have to interrupt my story, because seeing Jailor again reminded me of the time an engineer on one of the Okefenokee logging trains came after Perry one day and told him about seeing a bear "as big as a Brahmany bull" that had crossed the tracks ahead of his train. We put Perry's dogs on the fresh trail, but that bear dodged from one thicket to another all afternoon and never showed itself for even a fleeting shot. Finally, as he often did, Perry put himself in the bruin's padded soles and tried to guess what the animal would do next.

Leaving the armed engineer on the elevated roadbed, we went in the brush with Jailor and the rest of the pack. With me on one side and Perry on the other, the bear broke cover a quarter of a mile from the tracks, saw or smelled the engineer and ducked back into the thicket on the side where Perry lay in ambush.

It took two shots to down him, and then he ran half a mile before he collapsed. It was all the three of us could do to drag him across the swamp. We hauled him back to the logging camp on a flatcar. Then we weighed him in on the logging-camp scales at 615 pounds—Perry's record, by the way—and peeled off the widest black skin I ever saw.

i was chuckling to myself about that experience when Perry came out of the house with his shotgun. It was the doggondest gun I ever hope to see—an ancient, rabbit-eared, double-barreled piece with only one usable tube. Years ago one of Perry's boys stuck the barrel into the mud and ripped the iron into shreds when he tried to shoot out the clay plug. For many seasons Perry killed his bears through the one good barrel.

He called his dogs, walked off with his neighbor to the edge of the trees where the trail dipped into a gum slough, turned and waved to me. I had a strong urge to run after him and forget about that date I had in Waycross. But when Perry's neighbor told me the story later, I lived it as vividly as if I'd slogged over every foot of the swamp floor with them.

They soon found the heifer's carcass, and Perry turned his dogs loose.

"If I know bears," he said, "the old tub's lying somewhere close in these cassena bushes. He won't go far on a full belly."

He was right. In minutes the dogs jumped the big black. Crashing brush told the two hunters that the rogue had taken off for a long, wooded island just inside the swamp. It was the beginning of one of the strangest races the dogs ever ran.

"I got a good idee," Perry said, "that he'll make his stand somewhere on that island where he's headed."

He knew the bear's destination, but the bear probably knew Perry, too. It suddenly changed its course and took off at right angles to the island. It sloshed through knee-deep water that dragged at the low-slung dogs. And for an hour, it had even Perry running in circles. Each time the hunter guessed where the bear was going and plunged into the swamp to head him off, the bear changed directions. But as the shadows lengthened, the bruin turned back to the wooded island where Perry had predicted it would make its stand.

With his neighbor at his heels, Perry dived into the thicket. On dry ground, the tempo of the race changed. The dogs gained. The cold trail developed into a running fight that led through a patch of thorny bushes, across the slough that surrounded the island and into the pine and palmetto scrub of the high land.

The bear settled into a familiar routine when the race was nearly over. With the dogs snapping at his tail, the black would run 100 yards, climb a tree to rest, suddenly bounce off the trunk, land among the pack and start slapping right and left. Then it would run again.

By now the sun was almost gone. More by design than accident, Perry's neighbor dropped behind. Alone, Perry caught up with the animal in the last fringe of trees on the swamp side of the island. He broke out of a thicket within 15 feet of the bear. The rogue was slightly larger than medium size—about 400 pounds. It was clinging uncertainly to the rough side of an oak, 10 feet above the ground, and looking down at the dogs ringed around him at the base of the tree.

Snatching back the jack-eared hammer, Perry pointed his one good gun barrel at the bear's head. Just as he jerked the trigger, an excited dog lunged against his leg. Buckshot tore off the side of the tree. But the load hit so close that a couple of pellets ripped into the bear's shoulder.

The bruin fell out of the tree with a roar and landed squarely in the center of the dogs. With an infighting form that a boxer would envy, it went to work on the pack with short, hard thrusts. The dogs scattered. Then the rogue caught sight of Perry, standing 10 feet away in the dusk. It reared on its hind legs, then charged.

Perry snatched the empty hull out of his gun and tried to thrust home a shell that had become swollen in his wet pocket. He dodged the bear's first rush. Then, swinging the jagged gun barrel, he hit the animal a terrific smack that tore off half an ear.

The bear came on, and ripped and slashed until Perry's coat was in ribbons. Some blows cut through to his skin. Finally Jailor, sensing his master's predicament, rushed in and grabbed the bear's haunch.

taking advantage of the bear's momentary diversion,
perry plunged into the bushes.

Squalling with pain, the black swung away from Perry and slapped Jailor end over end into the brush.

Perry lost no time taking advantage of the bear's momentary diversion. He plunged headfirst into the bushes, drove the swollen shell home with the heel of his hand and poked his gun through the brush. When the black turned on him again, he blasted it full in the face and laid it out cold.

Perry's comment on the fracas was a simple statement of policy that he followed ever afterward.

"Ain't no sensible man," he said, "'ll tangle with a rogue bear after the sun goes down."

Perry Barbour gave up bear hunting 20 years ago. At that time the late Howard Coffin, looking around for a dependable swamper to help him protect his game preserve at Cabin Bluff, on the coast, offered Perry the job. He took it, figuring that he was getting a mite old for traipsing around the swamps looking for black bears. And, anyway, most of his good dogs were gone.

As a gesture to the kind of hunting he'd done all his life, he released the last bear he'd ketched alive and kept chained up in his backyard.

"I reckon," Perry said, "it was the only time I ever abused a bear that was minding its own business."

He grinned as he told me about it. It was one of the few times in his life, he confessed, when he'd drained a little too much stump water down his gullet, and he got to remembering about all the clothes and hide that bears had ripped off him, and about all the bears that had eaten his honey, chewed his pigs and run his cows until they were good for nothing but boot leather. He swaggered up to the chained black, stuck his face within leering distance and punched the bruin in the nose.

The bear punched back, twice as hard, and knocked Perry into a corner of the yard. The swamper got up and brushed off his coat. He pacified the bear with a glob of honey and unsnapped its collar. Then, with a lot more honey and a few well-chosen words, he tolled the black down the trail into the swamp and turned it free.

❖ ❖ ❖ ❖ ❖ ❖ ❖ ❖ ❖ ❖ ❖ ❖ ❖

SURF LOGIC - I know a surf caster who cut the hooks off all his lures with the explanation that for years the striped bass wouldn't bite when he wanted them to, so when the fish wanted to bite, to hell with them. - Dick Cornish, N Y DAILY NEWS.

POLISH EXTRACTION - Two anglers heading for shore got a warm reception from Game Protector Stanley Stefanick after he heard one tell the other in Polish, "There's a game warden standing on the dock; better hide that other string of pike." - Joe Beamish, SYRACUSE (NY) HERALD AMERICAN.

BLACK CROOK - Game Warden Charles Cochran of Limerick, Maine, was checking on illegal night fishing in a closed brook when he heard splashing sounds and spied a shadowy form scooping up a fish. "Stand where you are!" he shouted, flashing his light - on a large, hungry bear. Exit bear and warden, in opposite directions. - William H. Ridings, LAWRENCE (MA) TRIBUNE.

❖ ❖ ❖ ❖ ❖ ❖ ❖ ❖ ❖ ❖ ❖ ❖ ❖

taLL
But
SHORT

was fishing a high mountain stream when I ran into Caleb Duff. Caleb's a mountaineer from way back, but he loves to get a little news of what's happening in town, so I brought him up to date on a few things.

"By the way," I finished up, "someone stole the big bronze statue off the Elks' front lawn last week."

Caleb looked at me a long moment, then said, "I reckon not."

I must have looked annoyed at this contradiction because he hastened to add, "Now, this is confidential, but I'm gonna tell you about that elk statue. I got the story direct from the man that sold it to the Elks club 'bout eight years ago.

"That was a mighty cold winter up here in the mountains," he went on. "Usually it don't go no wuss'n 70 or 80 degrees below, but that year the bottom jest fell out of the glass. 'Twasn't safe for a man to venture out, and animals and birds was freezin' everywhere.

"Along toward spring this feller I'm tellin' you about found the elk. It was a big old bull that had been out foragin' and got its foot caught in a crevice. Before it could get free it froze solid. This guy had an idea—he was always a calculatin' sort of feller.

"He got some bronze paint and he gilded that elk all over. Then he lugged it down to town in a wagon and had no trouble at all sellin' it to the Elks as a solid-bronze statue.

"Well sir, it stood on their front lawn right up to this summer. But you know we've been havin' the worst spell of heat anyone can remember. Well, what happened was that elk finally thawed out, and jest walked off the lawn."

Steve McArthur

a racing jack turned my easygoing friends into the nearest thing to a war party this side of Hollywood.

Rabbit Hunt, Indian Style
by Jim Downs

the Navajo casually invited me to hunt jackrabbits, but i knew not what terrors lurked in the sagebrush.

PEOPLE HAVE GONE AFTER THE long-eared Western jackrabbit in every conceivable manner. Plinkers have stalked him, varminters have sniped him from a distance, ranks of shotgunners have driven him. The Paiutes netted him, and greyhound coursers and falconers have found him a beautiful quarry.

Archers, lines of people with clubs and, I suppose, little boys with slingshots have had a go at him.

But for pure catch-as-catch-can excitement and not a little danger, the Navajo Indians of northern Arizona have figured out a way to hunt jackrabbits that makes all other methods seem downright boring.

A Navajo rabbit hunt is a combination of English fox hunting, boomerang throwing, rodeo riding and just plain foolishness. It requires a horse that's at least saddle broken; two feet of juniper branch; and an utter disregard for your own, your horse's and your hunting companion's life and limb.

My introduction to this sport took place in the center of the Navajo Indian Reservation, about halfway between Flagstaff, Arizona, and Gallup, New Mexico. The reservation, as big as West Virginia, sprawls over almost 16,000,000 acres of Arizona, Utah and New Mexico. It contains a great variety of country, from tall, pine-covered mountains to sandy wastelands.

I'm presently an associate professor in the University of Arizona's department of anthropology. But in 1960, at age 34, I was a slightly overage graduate student at the University of California and was conducting anthropological research on the Navajo in the reservation's Black Mesa area.

This is rough country and was at that time remote, being 30 miles from the nearest paved road and an additional 100 miles to either Flagstaff or Gallup. The area's flat, sage-covered valleys and rugged ranges of dun-colored mesas were home to perhaps 5,000 Navajo.

The horse and wagon was a major means of transportation, though more and more pickup trucks were beginning to appear. The Indian trader's store looked and operated like something out of the 19th century. The main occupation, particularly when off-reservation work in agriculture or on the railroads was scarce, was and still is sheep raising.

The Navajo group together in outfits—that is, clusters of relatives living in hogans (cabins) within shouting distance of one another. The hogans center on the outfit's sheep pen. My wife and son and I were living in a hogan left vacant when one of an outfit's daughters and her husband moved off the reservation to work.

The Navajo are what anthropologists call matrilineal, meaning that a person reckons that he belongs to his mother's family, not to his father's. They're also matrilocal—that is, when a man gets married, he generally moves into a hogan owned by his wife and located somewhere near her mother's outfit. Husbands and sons-in-law don't count for much among the Navajo.

After we'd spent a period getting acquainted, one of the men in our outfit mentioned casually that there might be a rabbit hunt on the following Saturday and that maybe I'd like to join in. The standard Navajo invitation is always pretty vague so as not to appear to be applying any pressure on the proposed guest.

Navajo schedules are as vague as Navajo invitations, and the appointed time of noon came and went with only one eager hunter— me—present. By one o'clock, however, the men of the outfit had gathered under a brush ramada to wait for their neighbors to collect, some from as far away as 15 miles.

Horses were saddled and tied to convenient posts while the men, squatting on their heels and watching the far mesas, talked obliquely about the lack of rain, the price of wool and the goings-on of the neighborhood girls.

Since I had been brought up in the get-out-there-early-when-the-dew-is-still-on-the-grass school of hunting, a hot Saturday noon slipping slowly into afternoon hardly seemed the right time to go after any kind of game. My guides and hosts, however, shrugged off my concern and seemed pleased by the growing heat. By 1:30 that afternoon, half a dozen other hunters had ridden in quietly, tied their horses and joined the group in the shade. Finally, with a nod from Broken Foot, my host and the oldest son of the oldest woman in the outfit, the group mounted up and rode to the juniper groves on the flanks of the mesas.

It took another half hour to select the proper rabbit stick, a two-foot-long, slightly curved branch 1½ or 2 inches in diameter. One modern neighbor stood aside from all the cutting, trimming and peeling. He'd brought along his own stick—two feet of lead pipe.

Once the sticks were prepared, we mounted up again and rode toward the flat, sage-covered valley floor.

Modern Navajo seldom dress in velveteen shirts and knee-length Spanish-style trousers. A 10-gallon hat and ordinary off-the-rack work clothes have replaced the traditional dress. Older men wear clodhopper shoes, but a young fellow would rather be caught naked than to be seen without a pair of low-heeled, brightly colored cowboy boots.

A few of my companions still wore the traditional cloth turban instead of a hat, and a few others continued to wear their hair in the old style—a long club bound tightly at the back of the neck with white wool thread. A man can't do his own hair, so the condition of a Navajo's queue is a fairly accurate indicator of how much esteem his wife (and, in a few cases, wives) or sisters have for him.

Navajo horses tend to be tough and able to survive on a not-very-good range without grain and with only occasional bales of hay. Infusions of blood stock from time to time have produced a generally capable strain of working horses.

My own mount was the pride of the outfit, a big, rawboned, seal-brown quarterhorse fitted with a low-cantled association saddle. Some of the older men rode in handmade rawhide copies of the McClellan saddle. The Navajo adopted and adapted this army-style saddle after their defeat by Kit Carson and incarceration at Fort Sumner, New Mexico, in the 1860s.

Once the hunt started, the casual atmosphere disappeared. In the Navajo scheme of things, hunters must think of nothing but hunting and killing while in the field, or they will have no luck. My friends forgot the drought, the price of wool, and even the girls, and they thought and talked only of rabbits—past, present and future.

The party slowly spread out into a single line. Horses wise to the game, which included my own, began to pull on their bits and walk in mincing, excited steps, their heads and ears up and alert.

Broken Foot rode up beside me, nodded and said, "Good and hot. Rabbit don't run so hard." Having thus settled my misgivings, he rode off without telling me what in hell I was supposed to do with the stick.

I had played a bit of polo and imagined myself trying to do an off-side forehand smash on the head of a running rabbit with a two-foot stick from a Western saddle on the back of a 16-hand horse. Somehow, it didn't seem possible.

Then, in an instant, my unexcited, easygoing friends became the nearest thing to a real-life war party to be found this side of Hollywood.

Up ahead in the brush, a big jack, settled down out of the midday sun, became nervous and bolted, his long ears wagging as he dodged and skittered through the sage. Horses saw him and lunged forward without urging. The men began flailing their mounts with their sticks and calling out a high-pitched *Yip-yip-yip* that sounded like the hunting bark of a coyote.

Like most American boys, I used to beat my palm against my mouth and utter noises that, I was assured, were like those made by Indians. They aren't. Even when the occasion is the pursuit of an ordinary old jackrabbit, the sound of the Navajo hunting cry runs chills up your spine.

I felt sorry for those soldiers who had played the role of jackrabbit in front of Navajo war parties during the 200 years that the tribe was a dominant power in the Southwest.

Still wondering what I was to do with the stick if we caught up with the rabbit, I quickly forgot about Indian war parties and devoted myself full-time to staying aboard my mount. The big gelding was plunging straight after the rabbit, smashing through and leaping over sage thickets, sidestepping prairie-dog holes and dodging cactus patches and other horses.

In the horseback-hunt field, there are a number of gentlemanly rules about who rides in front of whom. On the polo field, the regulations about cutting across the path of another are very strict. Even in a steeplechase, there are a number of do's and don'ts.

But such refinements were not in force in central Arizona in the summer of 1960. It was every man and horse for himself, and all hands converged on the trail of the lamb-size jackrabbit without half a thought for anything else.

The Navajo set a great store on devil-may-care horsemanship. I knew I was being tested, so I simply hung on and let the big horse carry me where he would.

But I was still wondering about the stick. As it turned out, I didn't have to try any fancy polo shots. The Navajo had an even more difficult gambit. You *threw* the blasted thing!

At full gallop on a horse as excited as a flat racer just jabbed with a needle full of stimulant, you flung your stick at a running rabbit that never moved in the same direction for more than two jumps in succession. If you were a Navajo, you expected to hit the jack—or at least come close enough to scare him thoroughly.

The next 10 minutes contained some of the fastest and most exciting horseback action I had ever experienced, and I'd taken part in steeplechase, polo and fox hunting.

The jack tends to live and wander in a single area and even when pursued will not leave it unless pushed exceedingly hard. Our quarry hit the boundary of his domain after about five minutes of hard going, flipped head over heels and headed right back where he came from. By now his ears were laid back, and he was traveling flat out.

His reverse course took him right through the middle of the pursuing pack of hunters. Caught by surprise, the riders overran the jack, giving him 100 yards of grace before we were able to get back on his trail.

But even in the confusion, one young Navajo, with a plastic, flat-crowned 10-gallon hat and a flashy cowboy shirt with pearl buttons on the cuffs, came within inches of finishing our rabbit then and there. This wasn't bad, considering that he was throwing at a rabbit that was going one way while he was going the other, and he was trying to turn his horse at the same time.

We made three more hell-for-leather passes back and forth across the valley before the horses and men were too winded to go on. The chase was broken off, and the horses walked to the crest of a low sandhill. Covered with dust and foaming sweat, the animals blew and heaved while the hunters planned the final campaign against the jack.

From the surrounding brush came a dozen or so small boys on foot or riding on donkeys and horses too small or too old to keep up. Wide-eyed, they listened to the men discuss the chase thus far. The jack's every bound and change of direction was analyzed carefully and collectively. The men were beginning to understand this particular rabbit's personality and were anticipating where he would go to hide now that the chase had slackened.

After 15 minutes of rest, the hunt began again, the riders moving in line toward the sage patches where, the collective opinion had it, the jack was hiding.

The old hare wasn't surprised this time and tried to sneak away, moving a step at a time, ears low, body hugging the sand. But one of the riders spotted him and gave out a low, birdlike whistle. The line swung around and centered on the jack. Then someone let out a shout, and the whole thing started again.

The first chase had taken some of the steam from the horses and the quarry, but the rabbit was still able to lead us on two more sweeping, mile-long passes before he made his mistake.

Though pushed hard against the boundaries of his territory, he decided not to depart into unknown country. Instead, he turned sharply and tried to lose us by dodging back and forth in the thick sage. This gave the riders a chance to pull back from a flat-out gallop and anticipate his appearance in open spots.

He went down stone dead from three hits made at about 10 yards. The carcass was examined and passed to one of the trailing youngsters.

In good times the rabbit would have gone to the outfit's dogs. But in 1960 times were a long way from good in Navajo country, and fried rabbit took the wrinkles out of a lot of Indian bellies.

The second rabbit got up a long way in front and required hard chasing along the slopes of the mesas before we were within striking distance. Overconfident because of my success at having stayed with the pack during the first chase, I tried to throw my stick when the rabbit cut back and passed within five yards of me.

On the backswing, I knocked my hat off. The surprise caused me to jerk the reins, and my horse half reared. I saw the stick land 15 yards off target.

I looked around sheepishly, but no one was paying any attention, and the chase went away from me while I dismounted and got my hat and stick.

My next try was no less disastrous. Trying to avoid my brim, I misjudged the position of my horse's head and bounced the throwing stick off his right cheek. Having suffered this indignity, the big horse was none too certain about holding still when I attempted a throw, and he tossed his head defensively whenever I moved my right arm.

The third rabbit gave me a chance to redeem myself. It swung sharply to the right, causing most of its pursuers to override the track. I was somewhat behind the pack on the right and saw the big hare right in front of me. He was all mine, and I shouted something idiotic like, "I've got him!"

Using heels and stick with a vengeance, I drove the big horse toward the rabbit. The excitement made me forget the rules of the road in a Navajo rabbit chase, which can be summed up something like,

THE QUARRY WAS MINE, I THOUGHT, BUT THE HORSE
AND I DISAGREED ON THE TURN.

"Watch the hell out, buddy, here I come."

As I focused on the rabbit and readied myself for a real try at hitting it, a palomino blur cut into my range of vision from the left. A full-size Navajo on a half-size pony pushed onto the line right in front of me. He was oblivious of anyone or anything but the rabbit, and it was horribly clear that we were going to have a first-class horse smashup unless I did something.

With all my strength, I swung the big quarterhorse's head right. But he had sensed the problem even before I acted, and he chose to go to the left. I was set for a right turn, and the unexpected direction change catapulted me tail end over toes past the horse's shoulder. I did a kind of somersault in the air and landed flat on my back.

The Navajo whooped an acknowledgment of my ignominy and rode on. After all, we were hunting rabbits.

Sheer terror had caused me to clench my fist on the reins, and the sand was soft enough so that I didn't break any bones. Instinctively, I staggered to my feet in a shower of shooting stars and groped my way along the reins and back to the horse. After pulling my hat on and collecting the fallen stick, I scrambled back aboard, operating on the assumption that the horse couldn't be as dizzy as I was.

Among the Navajo, falling off a horse can be a very embarrassing thing unless one ignores it and gets back on right away. One of the few times I ever saw a Navajo parent strike a child was when a boy fell off his horse and cried about it.

My companions approved of my behavior, even if it was done in a semiconscious state, and named the spot Place-Where-White-Man-Fell-Off-His-Horse. But they didn't do it right then. If I'd broken my back, I doubt that they would have known about it until the rabbit was done in.

After that I chose not to push into the pack and was content to nurse a number of new aches and pains while galloping with a bit more care behind the remaining hunters. A number had dropped out as their horses tired. Others had started the 15- or 20-mile ride home before it got dark.

The afternoon slipped away quickly, and the hunt yielded three more rabbits before it ended—as informally as it had begun. We rode to a nearby water-catchment basin and rode the horses in, belly deep, to drink. Some of the riders who used saddles stripped them off and washed away the sweat.

The hunt was discussed in detail, and finally, just as afternoon was turning to dusk, the party split up and rode for home, each rider making a small cloud of dust to mark his passage in the wide, empty country.

I was sore, dusty, brush-scratched, stiff-armed and disgusted. I hadn't come within 15 yards of hitting a rabbit the whole afternoon. And that wasn't the end of it.

I hunted with the Navajo the rest of the summer and managed to throw my arm out more times than a rookie pitcher in spring training, but not once did I come within 10 feet of making a hit. My only rabbit was killed on foot with a single-shot 12 gauge, which I later traded for a handmade rawhide Navajo saddle.

The Navajo have been running rabbits this way since they began to steal horses from the Spanish in the early 1660s. But they also stole a lot of sheep and gradually gave up hunting as a main occupation in favor of herding. Today the sport of chasing jackrabbits is beginning to disappear.

The younger men of the reservation, like everyone else in the Southwest, from bankers to barbers, are enamored of the cowboy image. Rodeo is becoming the major summer sport in Navajo country. These shows are staged in arenas and corrals tucked away in the high steppe country. Horses and cattle taken from the range are used for the rodeos and then turned back to the range when the shows are over.

Fewer and fewer Navajo are driving the jackrabbit with the staccato hunting cry of the old days. Instead, they are hopping into pickups loaded with women in velveteen and satin and turquoise jewelry, and driving to Steamboat Canyon, Piñon, Rough Rocks, Blue Gap or some other romantically named spot in the Indian country to have a go at bronc riding or calf roping or bull dogging.

But there are still some who hunt rabbits in the old way. And if you want to try one of America's wildest sports and enjoy the company of men who don't give a hoot for anything but rabbits and risks, head for the Navajo Indian Reservation. There are still a few years left.

❖ ❖ ❖ ❖ ❖ ❖ ❖ ❖ ❖ ❖ ❖ ❖ ❖ ❖

faLse cast - A Syracuse carpenter swings a hammer all day without losing his grip, but his friends say that, three times in the past year, he tossed fishing rods into the drink after accidentally letting go of them on casts.
— Rod Hunter, SYRACUSE (NY) POST-STANDARD.

seeing eye dogs - Scientists say dogs can visualize moving objects at 2,600 feet and recognize their owner at 490 feet Some dogs we know prefer not to recognize their owner when he is 2 feet away. — Jim Wommack, GREENSBORO (NC) DAILY NEWS.

gulled - James A. Marsh, fishing at the mouth of the Russian River, California, left his bait can near the water's edge while he moved up the bank to eat his lunch. Gulls immediately swooped down on the can and began gobbling sardines. Marsh hustled shoreward to chase them. When he got back to his lunch, he found another flock of gulls making off with it — sandwiches, cookies and even the wrapping paper.
— Joe Dearing, SAN FRANCISCO CALL BULLETIN.

❖ ❖ ❖ ❖ ❖ ❖ ❖ ❖ ❖ ❖ ❖ ❖ ❖ ❖

taLL BUT SHORT

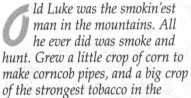

O ld Luke was the smokin'est man in the mountains. All he ever did was smoke and hunt. Grew a little crop of corn to make corncob pipes, and a big crop of the strongest tobacco in the country. Nobody else could smoke it. But Luke would set around all day and blow smoke rings. Strongest, most durable smoke rings I ever seen. Why, neighbors' kids used to gather an armful of them and play quoits all day long.

But the smoking finally ruined Luke's eyes–he couldn't see beyond the end of his pipe. That almost broke his heart, cause he had to give up hunting. But he wouldn't give up smoking.

One day he said to me: "I'd be obliged if you'd lead me up into the mountains. I aim to trap a bear."

I seen he wasn't carrying no trap, but I felt sorry for him so I led him up to a clearing that was his favorite spot for bear. "Now," he says, "aim me at the hardwood grove."

I done so. He stuffs his corncob pipe with tobacco and lights up. Then he sends a big cloud of smoke right across the clearing into the grove. In a minute we hear an awful huffing and puffing and coughing, and then out staggers nine bears, each one bigger than the next. They just stood there, plumb dazed.

"Aim me at the biggest one," says Luke.

I done so. Luke takes another drag at his pipe and then starts blowing smoke rings. And durn me if he didn't fasten them together so they made a chain! That chain reached right out and wound itself around the biggest bear. "Come on," says Luke, "pull!" And we drug the bear down the mountain.

It was dead when we got to the cabin—plumb strangled. Yes sir, old Luke got the biggest bearskin ever seen in the mountains—and enough smoked meat to last him three years.

James Meagher

"i wish i was in the army...i could gripe."

"hurry up, he may be playing possum!"

I Love A Quail Named Gambel

by Nord Riley

Pursuing the little bird that grabbed my heart, i Learned the pain of true devotion.

AT THE SALTON SEA, WE HAD, as usual, struck out. I hadn't fired a round. Leroy Younggren had shot a rare, miserable bird that was either a dwarf ruddy or a wet robin. By 9 A.M. we'd had it and started slogging in through the sea's peerless mud, a goop that for odor and consistency makes you think you're wading in Liederkranz.

"If I ever suggest coming down here again," I told Leroy, "have me committed."

Ashore, we renounced forever any attempts to hunt in southern California; we swore never again to be asinine enough to go after waterfowl in a desert. We changed into our slacks and short-sleeved sports shirts, shod ourselves in loafers, cased our weapons and began the 200-mile journey to our homes in Manhattan Beach, California.

An hour later, we had grown so sleepy from having been up all night driving down to the sea that we took a side road off U.S. 99, found some shade and flaked out. About noon we resumed the drive, heading north on the black-topped roads of the Coachella Valley south of Indio. Leroy drove, munching a candy bar. As I recall, he was prying a bit of peanut loose from a cavity when I cried out, "Good Lord, look at all those quail!"

Leroy got his elderly machine stopped after a while and managed to back her up. Twenty quail loafing on the bank of an irrigation ditch eyed us a moment, then jumped in the air and disappeared behind the bank.

"What'll we do?" Leroy asked.

"Shoot 'em!"

"I know that. I mean in our Oxfords? With high-base 4's?"

He wasn't arguing, he was discussing the situation while he tried to put his Lefever together faster than I did my Winchester pump.

Within 45 seconds we were clambering up the near bank of the canal. When we got to the top I laid eyes for the first time on the patch of desert where for the next 15 years I was to carry on hotly with a quail named Gambel. At our right stood a massive thicket, a triangular, gray-green fortress of greasewood 60 yards wide at the base, 100 long and rising to 40 feet in the center. Beyond it, spotted across a square mile or so of desert, were other thickets, some smaller, some larger. Between them was open desert, flat as a pool table, flecked with sagebrush and mesquite. It didn't look like much then, but that bleak patch changed the hunting habits of me and a dozen of my friends.

"There they go," Leroy said.

A plump, russet-chested, plumed bird dashed between two bushes.

LeRoy toLd me i Looked Like oiLveR HaRdy as i
gaLLoped HotLy acRoss the deseRt.

"How'll we handle them?" I asked meditatively as I watched it go.

"Charge 'em," said Leroy.

Charging is one way of hunting these quail, undoubtedly the most
popular. We plowed down the soft inside bank of the ditch, sank
sock-top deep in mud lying beneath grass on the bottom, grunted
up the far bank, down the other side and out onto the open desert in
full cry.

Ahead of us, the astounded covey began picking them up and laying
them down.

"Cut 'em off at the thicket!" I roared.

We went into our sprint.

A bird leaped up from under my right heel and whizzed off like a
rocket for the greasewoods. I stopped, turned, fired and was
absolutely amazed to see it fall. Leroy's double went off, followed by
his victory cry. I trotted over to retrieve my bird, and quail began
popping up around me like fat toast. One did what these quail are
always doing to me—he made me shoot him so he fell in the thicket.
Another flew off to my right no more than three feet off the earth,
sashaying through sagebrush. When I shot I got a small puff of
mixed feathers and sage, and the quail came down running. That's
another caper I've developed with Gambels: I'm forever having foot-
races with wounded birds. Leroy, who is an advertising man, said
later it was like watching Oliver Hardy as I went hightailing it over
the desert in my slacks and loafers after the cripple. The pattern of

my pursuit hasn't changed any over the years, and I get as many laughs as I always did. The quail beats it over to a shrub, hides until I catch up, then legs it out the far side to the next bush. All this time he's too close to shoot and too far to grab. When I finally nailed this one and returned, Leroy was searching for a bird.

"You're kind of a rapid old party when you get your steam up, aren't you?" he said. "I enjoyed that."

"How many did you get?"

"Three, including this." He held up an empty quail. "High-base 4's at 20 feet with my left barrel. Most of his parts are missing."

I found my first bird neatly laid out on a bed of sand and began my retrieve of the second, the one that crashed in the thicket. I could just spot him lying on his back 10 feet in. I plunged into the thicket. I plunged right out again, too, howling. This was my first clash with greasewood, and I retain the little white scars. Greasewood is a terrible plant, a dense, vicious, twisted growth rather like a tall porcupine. It has thousands of hard, long, sharp thorns that pierce your hunting clothes and open up your body. This first time I came out looking as if I'd lost to a leopard. I had a dozen red wounds, torn slacks, lacerated loafers, and my hat was hung on a thorn. I left it there to mark the body until I could stop crying.

We hurried on. At a thicket near a grove of date palms we located another covey. This is an odd thicket; it has a hole in the middle. We heard this covey deep in the thicket making their peculiar little babble.

"Listen to them in there," I said. "There must be 100."

"They're chortling," Leroy said. "They know we can't come in and they don't have to come out. We're whipped."

For a while we circled the thicket trying to shoo them out. We failed. Then I found a small thorny corridor into the hole in the middle. Once inside I stood in an open place about five feet in diameter.

"I'm inside," I called to Leroy.

"That's great, Riley. Thrash around."

"In thorns?"

"Thrash around to the northeast and I'll shoot 'em as they come out."

About that time the quail began to crash out of the thicket. We could hear them ascending through the greasewood.

Inside the thicket, I ran around in small circles like a desperate squirrel, trying to see just one quail. "They're coming out!" I cried.

"Where?"

I don't see why he bothered to ask. Gambel quail always come out of the side you can't see. Forty birds flew out of that thicket and Leroy saw none. I saw one. He spiraled up through the greasewood and out the top, 30 feet up. I caught a glimpse of a chestnut missile and fired.

"Hey," Leroy said, "not bad."

"I got him?"

"Certainly. I can see him. He's about six feet inside these funny-looking trees. Shall I get him for you?"

He didn't, of course. He put one long leg in and pulled it right back out. He profaned the desert air for quite a while, then he remarked, awed, "I'm bleeding in five places."

The bird was extracted by a stratagem I've used since. I cover myself with as many layers of clothes as I can borrow and have Leroy lift with a stick as many thorny branches as possible while I slither in on my belly.

From there we went on to other thickets and other coveys. The area was rich with birds. In an hour we had our limits. It was the beginning of my love affair with the Gambel quail, a cocky, crafty, brave little bird that I prefer to all others.

as a youth I was infatuated with a North Dakota prairie chicken. Later I had a series of affairs with pheasants, with sharptails, with

Hungarian partridges, all the time keeping steady company with mallards and honkers. When I moved west, I met the California valley quail and took up with her. But on that day, 15 years ago, the Gambel quail grabbed my heart and ran off into the greasewoods with it. And every year my affection for this bit of desert dynamite grows.

He is a handsome bird, blue-gray on back, his head decorated with red, white and black, his breast a glowing russet. Beauty is not much of an asset out in the harsh, hot desert, where pickings are slim and predators are all around. He has to be hardy, fertile and resourceful to survive, and he is all of these things. In the areas where we hunt he seems more populous than ever.

One thing that saves him is his extreme deceitfulness once he knows who you are and what you're after. He could show a fox a feint or two. The season usually opens in the middle of November, and by the middle of December a veteran Gambel quail can drive an ordinary hunter into a froth of frustration. Al Purvis, my brother-in-law, won't put up with it anymore. He refuses to hunt them in December.

A dozen times I've heard Al cry out in outrage from the other side of a thicket, "Did you see that? They're doing it to me again!"

"Doing what?"

"Deliberately flying quietly."

For some time I thought he was exaggerating, but not anymore. Normally, a Gambel blasts off at your feet with a whir that is the most exhilarating sound in hunting. Not in December. I'm prepared to swear that I've seen dozens of them ease off to my right, my left— or, more often—my rear, and then into the air with the silence of little owls.

"That does it," my brother-in-law says then as he marches back to the car. "If they're not going to whir for me, I'm not going to shoot them. They're not giving me a fair rattle."

People who have never hunted the Gambel quail regard him as disreputable. They're convinced he does nothing but run, that gunning for him is in the nature of a track meet and that to bag one is to ground-sluice one.

They do run at very high speeds, especially early in the season or in areas where the cover is sparse, and I don't know how many miles I've put in chasing them at full throttle. But they don't run all the

BY stomping, hollering and throwing things, we put
brush-hidden birds in an intolerable position.

time, or even most of the time—not the way we hunt them. There's a
style to the sport, and once you have it these desert quail will flush
for you when you want them to and where you want them to more
often than not. Nineteen out of 20 of our birds are killed in the air at
ranges never over 50 yards, with 15 being the commonest. I find
Gambel quail much less exhausting to hunt than the California valley
quail, which have to be chased up and down brush-covered canyons.
Gambels are generally out on the flat, open desert.

Over the years, we've learned how to hunt these desert quail in this
particular patch. We don't charge them anymore, not because we're
older and fatter, but because it's often futile. Fleetness isn't required;
patience is, though, and a slow pace.

One man can't hunt Gambel quail successfully. They simply dart into
a thicket. If it's a small thicket, they run through it and out the other
side and into the next one while the hunter is puffing up to the first
one. If the thicket is large, they stay inside and trot from one side to
the other as the hunter circles the perimeter.

Two men can handle them effectively. We get one on each side of a
thicket and, keeping abreast by hollering out our positions to each
other, stroll down the length of the greasewood jungle. We don't just
holler; we stomp, we hurl dead branches, herding the quail before
us. At the far end, if everything has gone right, we have the quail in
an intolerable position—a cul-de-sac. They've got no more cover for
footracing, and there's no place to go but up.

The old hands there in the bushes don't panic, however. They pretend they aren't there, and the hunter who doesn't know this trick often continues on to the next thicket. We wait, knowing they're waiting. Fortunately, men have stabler nervous systems than birds, and three or four minutes is about all it takes to crack a quail's composure. When he goes to pieces, the action is wonderful. Birds explode out of the greasewood like shrapnel. Some fly low, some go straight up, some curve back, some will fly right by your twirling head. This is no place for a duck gun. Since I had the old Winchester's barrel lopped off to 26 inches and a variable choke put on it, I don't miss quite as often as I used to. Nevertheless, if you can get one Gambel for two or three shells, you're doing well.

If two men are good at handling these birds, three is best. We have the third man circle widely and post himself about 30 feet out from the far end of the thicket before we beat it. With him out there, birds that decide to hoof it to the next thicket before we draw near are in some peril of being potted. The first time we took my old gunning partner, Dick Brunnenkant, down there, we installed him at the far end and told him to stay there while we shook down the greasewoods. We executed the maneuver perfectly and the quail began pouring out the far end, but Dick wasn't there. We found him later, wandering around by himself.

"I thought it was another one of your tricks," he explained. "Like snipe hunting with a bag and a lantern."

I must admit that much of my affection for Gambel comes from having hunted him in this bit of desert Leroy and I stumbled on 15 years ago. If I had only one place to hunt, it would be there. It has quail, doves, occasionally a pheasant, coyotes and rabbits. Wild and woolly things occur here, though that would seem impossible in the lush Coachella Valley, a few miles from Palm Springs. The patch is rimmed with date palms, with fields of cotton and citrus orchards, and a heavily traveled macadam road goes down one side. Yet the moment you set foot in it, you are hunting an area as old as time. The Gulf of Lower California once ebbed and flowed over this land, and when it retreated it left its dead behind—millions of seashells. Then the Indians took over, and, nicest of all, they still have it.

We don't jump any Indians whilst barreling through the bushes after quail, though we do pick up arrowheads and stone implements. What we have flushed is a goodly number of Mexican laborers who have sneaked into the United States. There are half a dozen of their camps in hollowed-out thickets, and in them they have cooked and eaten and slept under about the same conditions as Indians did years ago. The only difference is the Indians weren't being chased by the immigration people.

The first time I walked around a bush and pulled up nose to nose with a swarthy, brown-eyed man with a black mustache, I had to overcome a strong inclination to bolt.

"Well, well," I said finally. "Buenos días, eh?"

"Buenos días, señor."

I waved my shotgun in what I considered an affable manner, and he put his hands up.

"No, no," I said. I threw my gun to my shoulder and pretended to shoot a quail. He fell to his knees and mentioned the Holy Mother.

"I'm not reaching you, am I?" I said. I pointed my gun at him. "Hombres, no; pájaros, sí. Pájaros jump up—bang! bang!—that's all."

"Pájaros?"

"Sí, pájaros. Honest."

He beamed. I beamed. I gave him my apple. He thanked me. I went on my way, and he went back into his bush.

We don't have the Mexicans down there we used to, but the drama remains high. Last year, when my brother-in-law and I pulled in, a sheriff's car was already there, and two deputies were poking around in roadside bushes.

"You guys can't hunt here," one said.

"How come?"

"Double murder over there last night," he said, pointing to a house about 300 yards away. "We haven't found the second body yet."

As he spoke, a posse of 12 mounted men carrying side arms and walkie-talkies clattered up, followed by two more cars full of cops. Al and I were surrounded.

"I'm getting back in our car before a horse steps on me," I told Al.

A fellow with a badge, a .38 revolver on his hip, a sombrero and a hard, blue eye sauntered over to us.

"Hunters, huh?"

"Yes, sir. We just got here."

"You can help."

"Help?"

"Look for the body. He probably hid it somewheres around here. Look in all those greasewoods out there. If you find it, don't get excited. One of you stay with it while the other guy runs and gets us. OK?"

Al and I loaded up and started off. I stopped, came back and tapped the head man on the shoulder. "You forgot something, sir. You told us what to do if we find the body, but you forgot to mention what we do if we bump into the murderer."

"Don't worry," the man said. "We think we've got him."

They thought they had him. That's not enough for a natural coward. We didn't find the body—they found it a mile away—but neither could I hit a quail all day.

SINKING FUND - A skiff from a Point Judith porgy boat had just set out a purse seine when the boat started its motor. Apparently startled by the sudden noise, a huge school of about 100,000 pounds of fish made a mass dive for the bottom, taking skiff and seine with them. - Leo C. Dotolo, WESTERLY (RI) SUN.

BAND RETURN - Whoever owned a parakeet wearing leg band NO. 32070, NBA-56 might be interested to know that Dan A. Dahl of the Euclid Rod & Gun Club found it in the stomach of a 2³/4-pound black bass he caught at Fenelon Falls, Ontario.
- Hank Andrews, CLEVELAND (OH) PRESS.

DEPUTY - Ben Anderson, northeastern Ohio law enforcement supervisor, has a young retriever that circles the blind or brush when Ben is checking hunters. The dog retrieves any over-limit birds to the man who tried to conceal them but left his scent on them.
- Louis E. Gale, CLEVELAND (OH) PLAIN DEALER.

"**N**ever believed in no trophies," said the old trapper, spitting in the corner. "Meat's for eatin'. Ain't no head wuth nailin' on a wall."

"Well, how about that one?" asked the sport, pointing to a grizzly head on the cabin wall. "Biggest I ever saw."

"Never put it there," said the trapper. "And never figgered it was wuth the trouble of takin' down."

The sport, sensing a story, remained silent.

taLL but shOrt

"The winter five years ago was wicked," the trapper went on. "Colder than any I ever seen in the Yukon. Wuss'n that, there was no game for winter meat. That-there bear killed all the animals he could reach, during the fall, and druv the rest outa the country. Got so, after a while, that all I could shoot was birds for mulligan. And soon I didn't have a bullet left.

"Then a real cold spell set in. Hardly dared step outa the cabin, let alone run my traplines. Allow I'd have frozen solid within 100 yards. I shore was desperate. No food left, and no chance of gettin' any.

"You know, that cold got so bad that it woke up the bear outa his winter sleep. One day, when I dashed outside to get a bucket of snow for water, I saw him gallopin' toward my place. I knew what he was up to—he was figgerin' on takin' over my warm cabin. But he made a turrible mistake."

"What happened?"

"Why, when he reached the cabin he saw the chimbley pipe sticking outa the hole in the wall. He reared up so that his head was level with it, and batted out the pipe. Then he stuck his head into the cabin through the hole. Got stuck there. And there he stays."

"But what happened to the rest of him?"

"Froze solid in two shakes of a lamb's tail. And I had prime meat for the rest of the winter!"

Stephen Mack

148

"Looks Like aLi Haδ a pretty successfuL HuNtiNG trip."

"wHat pLuG you usiNG?"

A Down East Tale:
Bareback on a Bear
by Norman Jolliffe

if you want a challenge, take a long, heavy bow, sit on a tree limb and try to shoot a bear that's sniffing directly below you. i did. and that's when the excitement began.

ONCE I WAS ON THE back of a large, live black bear. My position was precarious, and I didn't stay on the critter long. The whole business was an accident, but I actually have ridden a bear bareback.

I was hunting for a bear at the time—no bear in particular, just any bear. Two friends were with me, not when I was actually riding the bear but soon afterwards. They also were hunting bears, and they too would have been happy to take any bears that came along. Any bears, that is, except very small ones or females. How you can tell a female bear from a male bear unless you can get up really close is beyond me, and I am a registered Maine guide. I used to think that, seen at a distance, male bears had an air of macho about them and that female bears acted daintily. That was my rule of thumb for guessing a bear's sex. My records proved I was 19 percent correct.

My two friends are highly placed in the guiding hierarchy of Maine, and they are careful about not jeopardizing their

reputations. Right after this bear-ride episode, they would have signed an affidavit testifying that it happened just the way it did, but today it would be hard for me to get them to do it. So I've decided to speak out and tell the story myself. I won't use the right names of my friends. Instead I'll call them Aristotle and Lucifer.

"Is this where it happened?" Lucifer asked me when he and Aristotle arrived at the scene. His false teeth were back at camp in a glass of water, so he showed mostly gums.

"There's apple trees down below there," Aristotle said. His knowledge of horticulture and his ability to identify plants amazed me, though I think I must have been particularly ignorant at the time. Aristotle was drinking (yes, boozing as we were hunting), and he was stumbling. He'd poked Lucifer twice with a broadhead—the day before yesterday and yesterday.

In those days—quite a few years ago now—Aristotle's favorite beverage came in a uniquely shaped bottle. His mother even fashioned a leather holster so that her boy could wear a bottle on his gun belt. His .44 Magnum hung on his right hip and his favorite booze on his left. Everyone in Aristotle's social circle was impressed. Now he is a teetotaler, having found out, contrary to his expectations and hope, that alcohol and profit in the guiding business don't mix.

Aristotle also smoked a pipe. Lucifer and I followed him, stomping out the fires he started.

"Ah, here are some old bear droppings," I said.

"Oh, yeah," Aristotle said.

"Yess," Lucifer said.

"With chokecherries," Aristotle noted, poking the droppings with an arrow. "See the seeds."

Those were glorious days of finely crafted, heavy recurve bow. In fact, when his recurve was new, Lucifer took it to bed with him. Lucifer's odd behavior is sort of a holdover from his childhood.

"Don't you use inserts with your broadheads?" I asked Aristotle.

"I have some with and some without," he replied.

"Here iss more droppings," Lucifer said.

"What's in them?" Aristotle asked.

"More seeds. And here iss a worn path."

Lucifer was excited. He waved his arms like a traffic cop, and because Aristotle had swayed close to Lucifer to contemplate the droppings, his pipe was knocked from his mouth. It flew into a prickly bush and started a fire.

I jumped onto the bush, put out the fire and managed to break Aristotle's pipe.

"Fletching glue might fix it," Aristotle muttered, looking at the three pieces of his pipe.

"I was up this tree over the path," I said, getting back to business.

"Yess," Lucifer said.

"Oh, yeah," Aristotle said.

"See the broken limb," I said. The limb was obvious, so I didn't point at it.

"Where?"

"Where?"

So I pointed to the broken limb and again explained exactly what had happened. Nothing about my bear ride was complicated or hard to understand. It had just been an accident—an accident that resulted in my riding a bear, holding tight to its neck. Undoubtedly I had ridden with the wild hope that I could choke the beast to death or at least limit its air supply to slow it so that I could dismount gracefully. And if not gracefully, at least uninjured.

Anyway, I had found the bear's droppings, the apple trees, the path, and the tree by about 4 P.M. I climbed the tree and sat on a thick branch. Now, a thick branch might seem comfortable at first, but two hours later my buttocks were sore and my legs were numb.

Suddenly a bear appeared right under me. I forgot my discomfort.

I drew back my arrow and waited for the bear to pass by, but it stayed under the tree. My bow was a recurve—a 58-pound Super Kodiak 64 inches long. I was holding all 58 pounds of pull. And nobody can hold that for long. I surely could have used one of today's compound bows. If my bow had been, say, a 58-pound compound with a 50 percent let-off, even my grandmother could have held it. She could hold 29 pounds provided, of course, I helped her yank past the peak weight of 58 pounds. I imagine Grandma could hold 29 pounds indefinitely.

My black bear was saying something to itself. It was sniffing around the base of my tree and woofing. Evidently, it had detected my scent and wasn't too happy about it.

I was still holding at full draw a 29-inch aluminum arrow on my 58-pound recurve. The bear stayed under the tree.

If I had suspected that compounds were not going to be invented, I would have invented one right there. With great stealth and quiet, I would have hacked lengths off each limb, screwed on wheels rigged with cables and made adjustments to the bowstring. Then maybe I would have been able to bend and shoot directly down. Certainly I couldn't do that with my long, unmaneuverable recurve. My elbows had nowhere to go, and if I tried to shoot, the bow's upper limb would smash against a branch and the lower limb might alter my anatomy. I suppose I could have tried to shoot by holding the bow with my feet. A bowhunting friend from Massachusetts says he sometimes shoots at game that way.

The bear was still woofing. *Woof!* it said, for perhaps the 10th time. It sounded like a dog with laryngitis.

In those days, I wore sneakers when I bowhunted, and sometimes heavy socks over the sneakers. In the fall I would saturate the sneakers and socks with deer scent. By the time archery deer season came around, my sneakers and socks would be good and stinky. A tiny bottle of the scent cost me $4.99 from Keith-the-Thief, owner of the local archery shop. Keith visited archery tournaments, selling his scent and other items from the back of his rusted pickup. When he wasn't at a tournament, he was out, with a funnel and hundreds of empty tiny bottles, stalking his pet deer (he kept seven). The scent was popular, and Keith promoted it well, sending free samples to outdoor writers and the like.

Obviously the bear was sniffing Keith-the-Thief's scent on my sneakers.

A bear's keenest sense is its sense of smell. It can't see well, and its ability to hear is only fair. But when a heavy, aluminum hunting arrow rattles against the sight window of a 58-pound hunting bow, a bear hears the rattle and starts to move away fast.

My arrow started to rattle, and my strength was fading fast.

Suddenly the limb I was sitting on broke. The arrow flew off, and my bow and I came tumbling down, straddling the bear's back. The bear's legs were moving, but the bear itself had not moved—that is, it had not overcome inertia. Obviously I had overcome inertia faster than the bear had.

Under such circumstances, it's difficult to judge a bear's size. But I fit well on its back, and my feet didn't drag on the ground. Its fur was thick enough though not especially long. To hold on I had to grab the fur on the bear's neck, and I had to drop my bow.

"How did you got off him?" Aristotle asked.

"I can't say exactly," I said.

"Dist you hurt your bow?" Lucifer asked.

I had inspected my bow. There was dry blood on it from my nose. The only noteworthy injury to anything had been to my nose. So I was having trouble breathing, and I'd lost the arrow.

"The bow is OK," I said.

"You have to be careful sitting in a white cedar tree," Aristotle said.

I got out a Band-Aid. We all were very matter-of-fact. But I could tell that Lucifer and Aristotle wished they had had my experience—although Lucifer has recently developed a good moose story he tells mostly at meetings of the guides' association, and Aristotle unwinds a rather exciting deer yarn when he has milk and cookies with his hunting clients.

"Yess," Lucifer says to the assembled guides. "My client is sitting straight, and his bow is bouncing on his knees. My diesel 4x4 is lugging along up the mountain trail when we see a moose. Two mooses! Three mooses!"

But I will let Lucifer tell his own story—when he finally decides to speak out.

Butt and take - An Iowa raccoon hunter told me he broke his hounds of chasing deer by penning an offending dog in a barn with a goat, an animal with a foot scent and attraction similar to those of a deer. After being butted from end to end of the place for several hours, the dog usually wants no part of a deer anymore.
- Ries Tuttle, DES MOINES (IA) TRIBUNE.

Backtracking - John Mooney encountered a hunter dressed in flaming red cap, jacket, pants, boots, shirt and even a red necktie who was carefully following a set of day-old deer tracks . . . backward.
- Theodore Giddings, PITTSFIELD (MA) BERKSHIRE EAGLE.

Stack-up - Tennessee biologists Roy Anderson, Sumner Dew and Jay Hammond saw two mallards collide in midair as two separate flights of ducks swooped down to some decoys. Both fell – one dead, the other stunned. The dead bird showed no shot marks, only a bruised chest.
- Paul Fairleigh, MEMPHIS (TN) PRESS-SCIMITAR.

taLL
BuT
SHORt

*S*ome says that necessity is
the mother of invention,
but I say that laziness is.
*Take my grandfather. He lived
out West when the skies were
full of tender, juicy pigeons.
Grandfather always said they
were a blessing. Why, in them
days there'd be millions of
birds in a flock, and they'd blot out the sun for a whole day when they
passed over his place. Naturally, Grandfather couldn't work in the dark.*

*He built himself a four-barrel shotgun. He figured there's no sense in going
to the trouble of aiming a gun if you don't get plenty of shooting out of it.
With his gun, he could knock down hundreds of pigeons all at once. Of
course, the recoil would throw his shoulder out of whack, so he'd take to his
bed for two-three weeks.*

*Well, one year game was scarce. No pigeons came over for a long time, and
the larder got awful low. Grandfather finally had to take his shotgun and go
out after rabbits. He walked more than two miles and never saw a one. And
then, all of a sudden, he spotted a big black cloud coming towards him in
the sky. Pigeons! Grandfather lets the pigeons get right over him and then
he lets go with four barrels. But he aimed a mite low and nothing came
down but hundreds of pigeon legs.*

*Grandfather went on home, a big grin on his face. After dark that night he
and Grandma went out to a hardwood grove back of the barn. They filled six
baskets with legless pigeons flopping around on the ground. Naturally, they
had tried to roost but couldn't manage without legs. That's why Grandfather
had shot low—he wasn't the man who would tote pigeons for two miles!*

William A. Miles

"why, he Left before dayLight to pick you feLLows up..."

"there, there. don't thank me. i'm Lost too"

Meat Ain't Everything

by Emmett Gowen

FHAD DECIDED IT MIGHT ADD TO the fun if my wife and I went out together on fishing and hunting trips. Her presence would contribute a primordial quality to outdoor adventure: She could be the squaw and keep the wigwam warm for the meat-hunting brave. Ugh.

Such fantasies can be pleasurable though silly. On the deer hunt it was to turn out that we were both innocents in the woods. "Imagine," Claire said later, "imagine sleeping in a bear's bed!" It's easy to imagine. Just remember how a wet dog stinks and then multiply that by a thousand.

We were allowed a buck apiece in the Tennessee Game Management Area of the Cherokee National Forest. Here the Unicoi Mountains constitute the back lot of the Smokies, that national bear garden with so many black bears that they come out to be petted by the tourists. One day a black bear got right into a convertible. The passengers stampeded out the other side. Then the wind blew the doors shut. The bear finished the tourists' lunch and became inquisitive. He began pawing things. He hit the horn, and it alarmed him. He came out through the top.

Now, in the state's managed hunts a deer permit entitles you to kill a bear, perhaps on the theory you should protect yourself if one tries to become intimate. But we were interested in venison, and the game census indicated that getting it in that area would be easy. Besides, when I had trout-fished here in the summer, a buck had kibitzed over my shoulder as I made my selection from the fly book. Perhaps, like my wife, he wanted to tell me something about fishing but just didn't know the right words.

my gun jittered all over and i jammed my elbow against a tree. not for a rifle rest— just to keep from falling down.

As with any man's deer hunt, this one began with plans and imaginings months ahead. I had my Old Brush Buster, a Marlin carbine in .35 Remington caliber. For Claire I acquired a more dainty .30/30. Not liking the grease-and-powder smell of a gun, she must have put some perfume on its cheeks. At any rate it got a scent somehow. She was supposed to practice on it and be ready. She kept putting off the practice until I got wise to her private intention of going along just for the trip.

I gathered that she dreaded the loud and vulgar noise a gun makes, shocking the ground squirrels and making birds flutter in alarm. She toted her carbine with pride, as something pretty, but didn't care which end she held it by. That didn't matter, except as a technical violation of the safety rule, for she never loaded it, never even had a notion how to load it. All right, she could hunt with a camera.

My car has one of those ingenious arrangements whereby the seat backs fall and permit the occupants to bed down comfortably at night. Its trunk serves as sort of kitchenette, with gasoline stove, fuel, lanterns, provisions, utensils, ax and tarp. The tarp, stretched between the car and convenient trees, makes a pleasant veranda. Rifles, camera and such precious items ride under the rear window behind the rear seat. Everything is really cozy, and in summer plastic screens keep out insects.

The first night in the forest we camped at a public picnic ground, arriving after dark. There was a big drift of leaves right where we wanted to camp. I kicked them to one side with my feet and in so doing kicked up an awful stink. We happily cooked supper on the gasoline stove while every now and then the odor bore in and made us wonder if we were in a nice, sanitary place. A wet dog's odor was a dainty perfume compared to that one.

"What in the world is it?" my wife wondered.

"Smells like a bear to me," I admitted.

This thought arrested her in the act of turning the steak. Glancing apprehensively about, she declared we'd better go back and stay at the lodge. I thought about it some more and became evasive. I wasn't sure it was a bear, after all. It was just a stink. Anyway, if we smelled a bear, a bear would, with his incalculably superior scenting powers, long ago have smelled us. He was probably back in the Smokies by this time.

I convinced her and she convinced me. She slept that night without a care in the world, while the thought of bears, coupled with overindulgence in steak just before hitting the sack, caused me to sleep lightly and apprehensively, with bad dreams about bears. During the night I heard rocks falling from the loosely laid wall around the parking lot, and then a chipmunk's screams. I could have suddenly turned on the car lights and killed me a trophy, except that both legal and sporting conceptions prevented. That bear seemed to know his rights.

Next morning, however, I examined the place and there was bear sign—still practically steaming. It was clear that a bear had adopted a summertime picnic ground for his lair, and that we, like Goldilocks, had slept in the bear's bed.

It was the big day now, legal to kill a buck. Usually when a man goes deer hunting, he has decided on some particular method. This method changes from trip to trip, as the sum of all his past experience changes. I intended to take a stand in one of several spots I had observed—a place just below a certain "top," or knoll, that was overgrown with laurel. There would be paths, crisscrossing in all directions, such as cattle make in going back and forth between barn and pasture.

I believed that if I stayed on stand there during the entire three days of the hunt, if necessary, a buck would be sure to come along. All the other hunters, moving about in the woods, would make the deer move. Every time some other fellow spooked one, I'd be waiting at a spot the deer might very well select to hide in.

It was going to take willpower to sit still in one spot for possibly three days, even for a fellow worked up, as I was, to the readiness to endure any hardship necessary to kill a buck. I wasn't sure Claire had that much willpower, though.

"You must be motionless and silent," I explained. "When you are still in the woods, almost anywhere, you are practically invisible. You know yourself that when anything moves in the woods it catches the eye. And any deer hunter knows if he stands still a deer may walk right smack up to him."

We found a nice place to put my wife on stand with the camera. This was at a drain down the mountain where a big hemlock stood. The spot was washed out into a dry pothole, which had caught a lot of leaves, and it was cozy. Under the big hemlock she would have shelter even from the rain that had come up. There was a maze of deer paths all around.

I took a stand nearby and sat there motionless for maybe 10 minutes. Then I climbed a little higher and remained still for a terribly long time—really long this time—maybe 15 minutes. Then I stalked around some, to get my circulation going, and remarked to myself that stillhunting takes more fortitude than any other sport. To be motionless all day is a form of torture. Anyway, I'd had enough, so I went back to see how my wife was making out. As I approached her hiding place, all was so quiet I thought she'd given up and gone back to camp. But no, she was there, being motionless. Talk about fortitude!

"I heard one walk right behind me," she reported happily.

"You heard one? Didn't you see it?"

"Oh, no," she said. "I couldn't turn my head to look without scaring it."

On the second day I decided that with the cold and fog and everything, it wasn't such a good idea for my wife to stay out there in a hole in the ground all day, motionless, and maybe catch her death of cold. So I left her at the checking station to take photographs of other people's kills.

In the dim, foggy light of the second dawn, I stood there under my stand tree, peering into the brush and the gloom, taking care when I turned my head to do it slowly. I watched to the right awhile, then slowly (and a good thing, too) pivoted my head back to the left. I saw a motion; I saw something brown. It was the flank of a deer.

The effect on me was incredible. Here was what I had waited for for so long and with such tormented patience, and now that it had arrived I was incredulous—felt that there must be some mistake. But I remembered to look for antlers. Soon, as the deer sauntered along, the rack came into view.

Rack? Why, it was a joke, a caricature. Deer don't have antlers that big! How could he get between the trees? Well, it wasn't worrying him. Nonchalance and serenity that buck had. He was a being in perfect happiness and health and fulfillment, and he was having a stroll in complacence and peace. And, he thought, security.

And then I began trembling. I couldn't get enough air into my lungs. In fact, I could hardly stand. There was no tree handy for me to take a rest on. The sights of my rifle leaped and jittered, and I could barely even point in the buck's direction.

Trying to draw a bead on a vital spot as the buck walked slowly along, I kept waiting for him to move out from between the trees. The situation was at once improving and deteriorating. For the deer, following the windings of the path he strolled, made a right-angle turn and came straight toward me.

My trembling was positively violent now. I was suffocating and palsied, having a siege of buck fever, that was for sure. Now I understood the ridiculous things other men have done in similar situations. I could now sympathize with the fishing partner who, having hooked and nearly boated a 50-pound catfish, carefully cleaned a shad for another bait, then tossed his pocketknife overboard and put the shad guts in his pocket.

I badly wanted a rest but the best I could do was sort of lean my right elbow against a tree trunk. That kind of rest would throw even an expert's shot wild. But I wasn't trying to hold my rifle steady: I was trying to stay on my feet. At that, there's an advantage to the prone position when you have buck fever—you can't fall down.

Somehow I managed to select two trees between which the deer would walk, and when he framed himself there I was going to shoot. I began trying to hold my point of aim between the two trees at least, but the front sight wobbled around over a large area.

When the buck got between the trees the best I could achieve was a sort of overall coverage, as if I'd been shooting at a rabbit with a scattergun. With the point of aim jerking back and forth in crisscrosses over the deer's head, neck and shoulders, it was strictly a snapshot. Anyway, I fired—and the deer simply dropped.

It was as if the spasm of my trigger finger had released what held him up. His head, however, remained erect, and he looked for all the world like a bedded-down deer alert for danger. I now had a jittery sense of elation, plus plenty of time for another shot, a calm, deliberate one to break his neck.

Instead I worked the action, standing there ready to throw the rifle up and shoot again. Thinks I, "If he starts to stagger up, I'll let him have it." Then he saw me.

The notion that he might stagger up became the second error. The first had been in not letting him come closer. The deer got up in a flash and from the first bound was in full tilt, running at right angles to me through all those trees. The emergency snapped me out of my jitters. This time I shot carefully, aiming at his right shoulder, leading a little. It was thoughtful and precise shooting in every way, the kind that lets you call your shot the instant you squeeze the trigger. I knew immediately that my lead had been too short and that the shot probably landed in the ham. Later I found a four-inch sapling splintered apart, and that meant a spent bullet by the time it reached its mark.

I worked the action and got off a hasty third shot that went wild. Just one flash of motion I saw after that, and the buck was gone.

Now, all I ever read had said: "Wait. Let him go somewhere and lie down and stiffen up." Was he badly hit? Bound to be. That head-on first shot couldn't have hit anything but neck, head, shoulders or chest cavity. Had it only grazed him it would have bled freely. There was no blood. It was a detective job now. One fact indicated the seriousness of the wound: The deer had not run uphill but down toward the road.

He had jumped right smack over the hole that had sheltered Claire the day before. Then he'd gone toward the road and vanished. And by his direction hangs the rest of my sorry tale.

I sat down and smoked and used up maybe half the time usually allotted for a deer to stiffen up. Then I set out to find mine. The fallen leaves were wet with fog, and I could track him by those he'd scampered through and turned dry side up. They made a plain trail, especially wherever he'd slipped a little in jumping over obstructions. I tracked him downhill until I could see the road and everything between myself and it. I was sure he hadn't crossed, because in the Unicoi Mountains the lazy and the elderly do their hunting by patrolling the road. There were two of them down there now.

The trail of disturbed leaves became confusing. In fact, there was more than one trail. I realized that fact after I'd tracked right back to my stand tree. Now, the deer hadn't circled back there, for that's where I'd waited for him to stiffen up. So there must have been another deer around this top just before I'd come out, and I'd become sidetracked onto a cold trail. I went back and tried to straighten out the confusion, but succeeded in complicating it by adding my tracks to the welter of them already in the disturbed leaves.

Next I started making circles around the area, doing it systematically, so that my eyes wouldn't miss a square foot of ground among the thickly grown second-growth saplings. I kept this up patiently all day, for my belief was solid that I'd mortally hit the deer and would find him. I didn't.

Lying awake that night I decided to spend my third and last hunting day on a careful investigation of the thicket between the road and the place where I'd lost the trail. The more I wore down the problem in my mind, the more convinced I became that my cripple had somehow hidden in that sparse thicket. Deer are cunning at camouflage. Maybe now he'd be dead and there would be an odd angle of his carcass to catch the eye. First thing next morning I walked resolutely toward the thicket.

Blam, blam, blam.

Blam, blam.

Amused, I thought, "The old boys sure have got that road covered with firepower."

I was so convinced my buck was in that thicket, either stiffened up or dead, that I searched it with all confidence. Those shots probably meant I'd driven a deer to the road hunters. Again I covered the thicket in systematic circles. I found where a deer had been lying down—my cripple, I believed. I ungloved and laid the flat of my hand on the leaves. I thought I could discern warmth.

All that shooting down on the road, I supposed, had jumped my deer. So for the rest of the day I searched for it, moving over the top into other thickets, taking long patient stands, listening and watching.

Once a doe and two fawns came within 10 feet of me. "Shoo," I told them. "I've mortally wounded your papa and gotta find him." The doe's chagrin and embarrassment when I spoke to her were worth the whole trip to see.

The only way I can account for my dumbness as a pathfinder was that a stillhunter stiffens up—in the mind. Those patient stands kept me numb, I reckon.

The facts of the matter didn't dawn on me until that night, when my squaw told me of an amusing incident at the game protector's checking station. "Two fellows came in dragging the same buck," she said. "Wow! Were they mad. One had hold of the horns—"

"Antlers, dear."

"—on one side and one on the other. It reminded me of two dogs having a tug-of-war over the same rabbit. Each of those hunters said he'd killed it."

"Where?" I asked.

"In the road, just below where you were hunting."

"Uh-huh. How many times had it been shot?"

THEY WERE LIKE TWO FURIOUS DOGS HAVING A
TUG-OF-WAR OVER A DEAD RABBIT.

"Twice."

"Where?"

"One bullet had gone into the chest cavity and on back through the entrails."

"Without expanding?"

"That's what John said." (John Lovin was the game protector.) I decided then I must change my brand of ammunition.

"And was the second shot in the right ham?" I asked.

"Yes. Why, yes. How did you guess?"

"The son-of-a-guns," I said, "fighting over a buck they found in the road."

"You mean you think they found your buck?" Claire asked.

"I sure do."

"Well, don't take it out on me, on account of the world isn't using you right. Don't get mad."

"At what?"

"Well, to keep those two hunters from fighting, John used diplomacy. He suggested they divide the deer. One took half the meat and the hide. The other took half the meat and the head."

"Why should I get mad at that?"

"That nice young warden helping John said something," Claire went on. "Now don't get mad. He said he bet neither one of them had killed the buck, or even hit it."

"Yes, yes. Go on."

"He said he bet your cripple came out onto the road and they caught it. Now don't get mad."

"I'm not mad," I said.

I was vastly relieved. I believed my buck had been found. I was glad I had guessed wrong after I'd run it out to the men on the road. Otherwise I'd have gone down there and got into the row. And how the heck can you divide a buck three ways?

aLL uNStRuNG - Lacking a rope with which to tie to their car the deer Ed Webber got with bow and arrow, Ed and his unsuccessful companion, Dave Young of Niagara, used the strings from their bows. So the first thing they saw as they pulled away was a 10-point buck in a roadside field.
- Bill Hilts, NIAGARA FALLS (NY) GAZETTE.

HiGHBaLL - Stopped by a conservation officer, a Massachusetts hunter with a heifer strapped to his car cheerfully admitted: "Sure I know it's not a deer, I didn't get one, so I bought this heifer. Here's the receipt. I'm having a ball. You're the fourth guy that's stopped me."
- Paul Lacaillade, MANCHESTER (NH) SUNDAY NEWS.

WHOO stuff - Wyoming Wildlife Magazine tells of the wise guy who joined a crowd attracted by an owl in the window of a taxidermy shop. "If I couldn't stuff a bird better than that I'd give up," he boasted. He had no further comment when the owl turned its head and winked.
- Theodore Giddings, PITTSFIELD (MA) BERKSHIRE EAGLE.

taLL
But
sHORt

Jake and Hobe and I were hunkered down on an old log at the edge of the woods, in a spot where we had a little shelter from the raw November wind, listening to the two redbones unravel a cold coon track in a field of standing corn a quarter of a mile away.

It was midnight now, and the coon must have come down right after dark. That track was really stale, and the hounds were making slow work of it. One of them would pick up a whiff of coon scent every once in a while, and tell us about it, and then for five or 10 minutes we wouldn't hear anything but the wind. Singer, the young bitch, quit two or three times, but old Drum kept plugging away, and every time he talked out she'd go back and try it over again.

"That Drum of mine is a great cold trailer," Jake remarked with pardonable pride.

"He's all right," Hobe said grudgingly, "but he can't hold a candle to my Nosey dog. What's the best job of trailin' you ever seen Drum do?"

"I put him down last fall on a track I knowed was 12 hours old, and he had the coon goin' in 20 minutes!" Jake snorted.

Hobe grinned tolerantly in the lantern light. "Any fool hound oughta do that," he declared. "But there ain't many like that Nosey of mine. He took a track all by himself, in my back pasture a couple of months ago. Worked on it for a whole week. Finally he barked up one night, on a big hickory down at the end of the lane, and I went down to see what he had. Danged if it wasn't the skeleton of an old coon that had crawled up there and died in a fork, musta been all of two years ago. Yes sir, I'm sure sorry that mink chewed Nosey's foot last week. I wish we had him along tonight!"

Weldon Gage

168

"we wuz aimin' to play tennis when the crick goes down."

"you could have given brother one of the blankets off our bed."

Tarpon, by Gar!

by Hart Stilwell

a Hilarious tale of anglers who lived in different countries—and kept getting in each other's hair

WHEN DAVE AND I ROUNDED THE last big bend before reaching the mouth of the Rio Grande—where it flows into the Gulf of Mexico—we saw two familiar sights. One was calculated to work on the systolic blood pressure, the other on the diastolic.

First we saw tarpon blasting at the surface—lean, racy silver kings slashing at mullet, sending spray high as they burst up into the air. The early-morning sunlight danced on their glistening scales.

Then we saw a tiny white sail on the water near the tarpon—a miniature sail that we knew was rigged on a miniature raft. It was the contraption that José Francisco Garcia, commercial gar fisherman, used for carrying his bait out to where the gar were. And to us and other Texans, José and his rig were the biggest nuisance along the river, and had been for years.

We had come to dislike José passionately. Many times we'd shouted at him, trying to drum some logic into his thick skull, only to have him shout back, trying to drum some logic into our thick skulls. Maybe we could have reached an understanding if we'd been able to sit down and talk in an ordinary voice. We couldn't—there was always at least a 40-yard space between us.

SOON everything was messed up into one wild, bouncing, lunging conglomeration.

For José fished from the Mexican shore of the river, while Dave and I fished from a boat near midstream. We were careful never to cross the center line of the river—never to leave U. S. "soil."

We communicated with José by shouting—so that he could hear us above the roar of the nearby surf—and by signs. When you shout, you seldom sound reasonable. As for the signs we exchanged—well, very often they weren't intended to be reasonable.

For José floated his bait out in such a manner as to have the heavy hand line always near us, always ready to gum up the works just as we were getting into the thick of battle with a tarpon. And we, on the other hand, were always stirring around, scaring gar away from his bait.

As nature would have it, the tarpon schooled up and fed on his side of the river, where the stream curves northward, and the gar gathered on our side, near a sandbar. We told him he should move upstream; he said we should. Neither moved.

So Dave and I set out to renew the old feud as we circled José's sailing raft, with the gar bait dangling from it, and eased up near the center line, within casting distance of the tarpon. They were feeding wildly, bouncing mullet in the air at times.

I tied on my big tarpon plunker, the most valuable material possession I owned at that time. It was during the war years, and that irreplaceable floater was the last of the Mohicans, the only one left in my box. I had lost the mate to it only the week before. Dave thought I ought to put the plug away and save it as a souvenir. But I can't resist offering a surface lure to tarpon when they are begging for one.

We glared at José as we eased up for the cast, and I guess he glared back at us; at that distance I couldn't be sure. At any rate, there were no friendly exchanges between us. Then my floater settled to the surface and Dave's underwater plug followed it down an instant later.

Wham! Wham!

When Congreve talked about the fury of a woman scorned, he had never seen a tarpon strike at the surface or he'd have changed his sweeping statement. There is nothing else exactly like that strike—the fish just seems to fly in every direction at once. And now we had two of them flying, for tarpon hit both plugs the instant they touched the water. The silver kings burst into the air as though catapulted by powerful springs. Dave's tossed the lure, but mine—a small one—got himself stuck and headed upstream, clearing the water twice in the process.

I hauled in the light anchor with one hand while holding my tackle with the other. Dave started the motor and began backing toward our side of the river. When you're fighting a tarpon from a 60-pound boat, it's a nice idea to keep plenty of space between you and the fish.

Then my tarpon ran under José's gar line.

I plunged my rod tip into the water, trying to clear the bait dangling from the raft. I couldn't clear it. The line caught on the gar hook. Then the tarpon reversed his field, and the gar bait, raft and sail were all messed up in one wild, bouncing, lunging conglomeration.

To a stranger the sight of the miniature raft and sail banging against the tarpon as he jumped might have been funny. To me it wasn't funny. "Get your infernal line out of my way," I shouted at José.

"Leave my line alone," he shouted back at me.

The same old exchange. José began hauling in his sailing raft, which meant that he was also hauling in my tarpon.

"Let my tarpon alone," I shouted.

José stopped hauling in and waited for me to do something. There wasn't anything I could do. Only a madman would have brought that mess up alongside a boat and tried to handle the tarpon.

"What you want him to do?" Dave asked.

"I want him to die," I said. I had to yell to José to go ahead and haul in. He yanked the tarpon onto shore, banged it on the head with a chunk of wood, then untangled the lines. When he was through, he tossed my plug back into the water, straightened up his rig and sent that infernal little raft sailing back past midstream, just above us.

"Fine way to treat a tarpon," I said bitterly.

"Forget it," Dave said. "He'll eat it—at least it won't be wasted."

"I wonder if we couldn't get the Customs to stop him," I suggested. "He's a commercial operator, fishing in American waters."

We returned to our fishing. After missing three or four strikes in rapid succession, Dave tied into something big and heavy only a short distance from the boat and down fairly deep. Tarpon sometimes indulge in the nasty trick of following a plug close to the boat before striking. They're likely to bounce right into your boat or smack you on the head as they lunge about. I hoisted anchor and began paddling like mad, but the fish continued to dog it down deep. Still, we suspected nothing out of the ordinary, since a really big tarpon that takes a lure deep often shakes his head and fiddles around for quite a while before coming up to the surface to see what's wrong. Then he gets boiling mad.

What finally came to the surface that time was an alligator gar about seven feet long. He surfaced and threshed about, opening his tooth-filled snout, trying to get rid of the lure.

From the Mexican side of the river there came a mighty shout. Now we really had something on the line, in the opinion of José. He registered calm indifference bordering on scorn when Dave or I battled a tarpon. But a seven-foot gar—that was meat on the line.

José splits the gar with an ax, takes out the meat along the tail and smokes it. In Mexico gar meat is called *catán*—it's considered pretty good eating.

Dave set to work to get rid of the gar so we could hurry back to our tarpon. They don't feed forever, and we knew the fireworks might stop at any instant. Ordinarily Dave would have cut the line. But plugs were scarce then. So I paddled him ashore and he got out and went to work. Twenty minutes later he maneuvered the ferocious-looking monster near enough for me to bang it on the snout with a pair of heavy pliers. I hauled the gar onto the sand with the leader, took out the plug and was about to shove the fish back into the river when Dave said, "Hold it. I've got an idea. Let's give it to José."

"Why?" I asked. "There's no poison in it, is there?"

"I'm serious," he said. "Let's make the first move toward an armistice."

"OK," I said. "But remember—this is your idea, not mine."

We tied a heavy cord on the gar's snout and towed him to José's raft. I secured it to the hand line and motioned to José, who was watching suspiciously, to haul it in. When he pulled that monster up on shore he acted like a man overcome. He waved to us half a dozen times and did a lot of talking, most of which we couldn't hear because of the noise of the surf.

Then, by way of appreciation, he moved downstream about 10 feet and sent his little raft sailing a lot closer to us. Dave looked at it in astonishment.

"You and your armistice," I said. "I guess you'd call that getting chummy with us?"

"How was I to know the man's insane?" Dave countered.

the tarpon were still striking, as I discovered the instant my floater touched the water again. A small fish got a solid grip on it and I slammed the hooks into him. He bounced high, rolled up in the leader and cut the line. On the next jump he pitched the plug free. It fell about two feet from the point of land where river and gulf meet on the Mexican side and started slowly on out toward the open gulf.

"Let's go get it," I called to Dave. "Hurry!"

"It's in Mexico," he reminded me,

"Who cares? That's the last floater in the world."

"We better not cross," Dave cautioned.

"I know," I admitted sadly. I was well aware that one boat crossing to the Mexican side, violating the terms of our river fishing, might end that kind of fishing for a lot of people besides Dave and me.

"Cast for it," I said to Dave.

"You cast, I'll handle the motor," he said, passing his tackle to me.

I dropped the plug all around the floater, but it was beginning to bounce as it moved out over a submerged bar into waves that were steadily increasing in size.

"I better not go much farther," Dave said.

"One more cast," I told him. Then I glanced toward the point of land on the Mexican side and saw José wading rapidly after the plug. He was in knee-deep water, then in waist-deep water. The waves were beginning to bounce him a little.

"Better go back," I shouted to him.

"I never thought you'd value a mere human life more than you do that plug," Dave said.

"I don't want his death on my conscience," I said. "Look, he's swimming."

José always wore light trousers cut off at the knees, no shoes and an abbreviated shirt, so his clothing was little handicap to him in swimming. He gained rapidly on the plug. Still, Dave and I were ready to make a run for him—regulations or no regulations—if he got into trouble.

But he could take care of himself. He swam to the plug, turned and swam back until he could wade to shore. We moved along parallel with him, still remaining on our side of the river. When he reached his old stand he started to haul in his raft, but I shouted at him to wait. I cast Dave's plug up on shore and José tied my floater to the line.

"Now let me suggest that you lock that infernal thing up to avoid temptation," Dave said. "It interferes with our fishing."

"Not while they're still hitting at the surface!" I declared.

I cast the floater out and hung the biggest tarpon I ever saw in the river. He was so big it took him two tries to jump all the way out of the water. Then he headed for the open gulf. We followed until the boat was bouncing like a cork. Dave wouldn't go any farther, so I clamped down. The line broke near the leader.

When we returned to our fishing spot I sat in the boat meditating upon the cruelty of fate. Tarpon were still striking, but for a moment I was in no mood to fish. I was mourning the late-departed plunker. Then Dave said, "Take a look at what's coming."

I glanced toward José and saw his little raft on its way out, coming directly toward our boat.

"What the devil's wrong with the man?" I said. Then I looked closer and saw something on the raft. Tied to its mast was a big red and white plug. For a moment I thought I was dreaming. I wasn't. The plug was exactly like the one I'd lost the week before. I pulled the raft alongside with an oar, untied the plunker and examined it. It was mine—I could tell it by its battle scars. Evidently it had drifted downstream and José had picked it up.

"Now I suggest—" Dave began, but I cut him short. "I'll lock it up," I assured him. And then I began doing salaams and bows toward José, shouting to him what a fine man he was—José, who had been our enemy for years. He was pleased. His white teeth sparkled as he grinned.

The tarpon were still striking, and luck began to turn our way. José moved upstream a bit, and Dave hung a flashy five-footer and managed to keep it clear of the raft. I ran him to shore and he beached the tarpon after a 15-minute battle. Then I landed a four-footer.

We were getting six or seven strikes for every tarpon we hung, and landing maybe one out of a dozen strikes, which is about normal when you cast plugs.

Then all action stopped. Dave tuned up the motor and we waved farewell to José and headed up the river toward our car. A mile or so upstream we passed a shallow mud bank on the American side, a place where gar frequently annoy us when we're trolling for tarpon.

Trolling in the Rio Grande, or any other tarpon river, is often the surest way of getting action. If you see the big fish schooled up, you can take them casting. If they're feeding actively, as they had been at the river mouth that day, they'll take a floater or an underwater lure worked near the surface. If they're farther upstream and merely rolling, your best bet is to cast a sinking lure and let it settle to the bottom, then barely move it. If they're not schooled up, just showing here and there along the stream, trolling often pays off.

But then tarpon fishing may turn into gar fishing, much to the annoyance of the angler. Gar strike freely if the water is murky, or if the angler trolls fairly fast. Gar like a fast-moving plug, although they aren't so particular about mullet, which they carefully cut off just back of the hook.

As we passed the gar flat, Dave said, "Let's catch José some *catán*."

"Fine idea," I said.

For an hour and a half Dave and I did battle with a kind of fish we ordinarily avoid as we would snakes. Those gar mangled our plugs, chewed off paint, bent hooks, wrecked leaders. But we used our oldest plugs, and the gar didn't mind the difference. We assembled seven fish on the bank, two of them well over six feet. We tied their snouts together, dragged them into the river and towed them all the way back to José's raft.

Then we tied them on without letting José see them and shouted for him to haul in. When he got it to shore and began to drag those gar onto the sand one at a time, I felt more pleased and excited than he did. You get a strange sensation when you finally break off an old feud and make a brand-new friend, especially if you top things off by doing a big favor for that friend.

José just stood looking at the gar and moving his head from side to side. It was a windfall for him, and I resolved that any gar I caught in the future would be tied onto his little sailing raft.

José motioned for us to wait for him. He went to his camp, where he kept a fire going to smoke the gar meat, and returned with a bottle. He sent it sailing out to us. It was tequila—the rugged "goatskin" kind that has a fierce bite to it. It is rough and thorny all the way down, and even after you get it down it sort of wanders around as though looking for a fight.

But Dave and I drank hearty toasts to José's health just the same. When we started to send the bottle back to him, he shouted excitedly, "No, a gift! Keep it."

We took off, happy in the thought that we had struck a resounding blow for better international relations. And we're going to fish that spot again for tarpon, by gar!

taLL BUT SHORt

Rusty McCann told me the story hisself. There he was on his Alaska trapline without a pelt to show for his work.

Provisions gone and not a cent in the poke. Rusty figures he can't starve, so he starts for town, carrying an empty barley sack. Weather was coldish, he says, about 80 below.

Night comes and Rusty crawls into a hillside den. Trouble is, there's a big brown bear in there, and Rusty steps on its paw. The bear rears up, hopping mad, and starts for Rusty. Without thinking, Rusty throws the sack over the bear's head and gets out of that den. And the bear right after him. It don't make a sound, which is strange, but tears around until it gets the sack off'n its head. Then it goes back into the cave.

Rusty picks up the sack and finds it's full of icy clumps. "What's this?" he says, holding one in his hand. Pretty soon it thaws out—with a loud snarl. Doggone if the sack ain't full of frozen growls, bellows and roars! Rusty totes them along to town and goes into McGonigle's Cafe. "Listen," he says to McGonigle, "I ain't et for days nor drunk for weeks. Set me up a drink."

"No," says McGonigle. "Put cash on the bar!"

Rusty drops his sack in a dark corner and goes out to see what he can mooch. He has no luck for half an hour, then hears a commotion up the street. Men come flying out of McGonigle's and inside there's a terrible roaring and bellowing.

"A brown bear is loose in there!" screams McGonigle. "A hundred dollars to the man who'll kill him."

Rusty knows the noise is coming from his sack—the roars are thawing out. So he goes into the empty saloon and helps himself to all the liquor in sight. After a while the roars stop coming out of the sack, but Rusty has a few more drinks anyway. Then he yells to McGonigle: "It's safe now!"

McGonigle comes in and says, "Here's your $100, Rusty—you earned it. But where's the bear?"

Rusty looks scornful. "Told you before that I was hungry," he says. "I et the bear."

Handlogger Jackson

"you'd think we'd at Least see a track!"

"ed must have got his second wind."

I'm Sick of Moose

by Eric Collier

i'm a tolerant chap, but after 26 years of dodging arrogant moose, i've had it.

OCTOBER WAS making shift to step aside for November. Three inches of fresh snow blotted yesterday's jeep track.

With luck, the snow might melt within a day or two, but then it might not. In the Chilcotin country of interior British Columbia, at the 4,000-foot level, a snowflake that hits the ground in late October might well be around come next April.

For the past 10 days, the hunting had been poor. We pounded the alder thickets on the hillside and the willow swamps in the valley for six days without seeing hair, hide or horn of a trophy bull moose.

The annual rut was over, the bulls were footsore and battle-scarred, and they didn't care a whoop whether they ever touched noses with a cow again. To get away from it all, they'd gone into hiding in the alder thickets and mazes of second-growth pines where you couldn't see an elephant bedded down 30 feet away.

So for six days in succession we labored in vain. On the seventh, when perhaps rightly we should have been resting, we blundered almost head-on into a bull with a 51-inch spread of horn. He was getting up from his bed in a clump of alders. You could have hit him with a peashooter, he was that close.

A sigh of intense relief whistled from between my teeth as my hunter let go a shot and the bull buckled and went down. Sheer force of habit compelled me to pummel him between the shoulder blades. "Good shooting!" I bellowed into his right ear, even though that bull was so close he could have brained him with a fence rail.

To me, the killing of that bull brought a finish to another season of guiding. Hence, the sigh of relief. Every day for the past six or seven weeks, my mind, as well as my flesh, had grappled with a single problem—locate a bull moose, then step aside and wait with bated breath to find out whether my hunter would put his .30/06 or other such lethal bullet into the vitals of the bull or into the flesh of a jack pine six feet away from the critter.

I've never stretched my guiding activities into November, though the moose season here doesn't close until December. I know when enough is enough. Besides, a more placid and less nerve-racking business offers a useful outlet for my natural talents when the winter's snow has come to stay and when most any morning you're likely to step out of the cabin door into an atmosphere made almost brittle by a 30-below freeze-up. The business is the trapping of mink, otter, lynx and other furbearers whose pelts some female in New York, Paris, London or elsewhere figures will look a heap sight better on her than on the animal that grew it.

Now, with some 600-odd pounds of dressed moose meat reposed in the back of my hunter's pickup, I lashed the horns securely to the front bumper, where all and sundry could see them without having to strain their eyes. As I was about to wish their proud owner Godspeed, he chanced to remark, "I suppose you'll soon be killing a moose for your own winter's meat?"

His words goose-pimpled my flesh. A look of sheer weariness clouded my eyes. Blood flushed my cheeks. Then, taking an exceedingly deep breath, I informed my paying guest, "Come freeze-up, I'll buy myself a yearling steer and a hog from some rancher hereabouts and butcher them out. With the beef and the pork, we'll have plenty of meat for the winter."

His eyebrows hefted. "Beef . . . pork!" he exclaimed. "You mean to tell me you eat beef and pork with all these moose bedding around on your doorstep?" He stared sort of pitifully at me and shook his head.

But then he knew nothing about that movie camera or of the other ill treatment I've put up with from moose since a day many years gone when I looked my first bull moose in the eye and wondered what sort of an animal is this. But it was the movie camera incident that soured me on moose from the start.

It happened in the fall of 1935. Prior to that time my dealings with moose had been strictly on what might be termed the frying-pan level. I shot one occasionally for meat, but no oftener than I had to. The carcass of a nice fat buck mule deer was far easier to handle. And in those days, there were plenty of buck mule deer.

We all make mistakes, and in the fall of 1935 I maybe made mine. I suddenly found myself bogged clear to the ears in moose with no one to blame but myself. No one compelled me to take out that guide's license; I did so of my own free will. The fact that a trapper like myself could maybe make an honest buck in the guiding business might have had something to do with the decision.

Anyway, I got stuck with the license, and on my first hunt as a professional guide I had in the hunting camp a financier from Vienna, Austria, a surgeon from Oslo, Norway, and a combined author-opera singer, also of Vienna. If they had been content each to bag a trophy bull and leave well enough alone, all might have ended happily. But among an assortment of excess baggage they brought was a cumbersome movie camera that had to be mounted on a tripod before it was ready for action. I didn't like the looks of that movie camera from the moment I set eyes on it. I made a swift mental decision that an Indian of the Riske Creek band whom I'd hired as an assistant should have the rare privilege of toting this white-man's burden on his own skookum shoulders.

But that Chilcotin Hiawatha had a mind of his own where movie cameras were concerned. Though he'd never seen one before, he stared broodingly at this one. He bore the load for exactly 25 minutes, punctuating the passing of each with a gutteral oath in his native tongue.

"Picturesque language," observed the surgeon. "But what does he say?"

"Heap fine camera," I interpreted.

Wriggling out from the packboard harness and dumping the camera on a boulder, the Indian said suggestively, "More better you pack." And when I tried to let on that I hadn't even heard him, he handed me an ultimatum. "S'pose you no pack, me I go."

And if back to his reservation he went, I'd be stuck a two-day saddle-horse ride from any sort of neighbor, with three moose-crazy hunters on my hands and no assistant guide. Which might have been OK with me, but not with the British Columbia Game Department. According to page so and so, section so and so, of the B. C. game act, an outfitter had to have one guide for every two hunters in his camp.

From that moment, I had all of the camera to myself. For 10 purgatorial days I bore that burden in stoic silence, wishing all the time that such gadgets had never been invented. Over windfalls and rocks, across muskeg and creek bottom, up hill and down dale. Wherever a moose left its track, I and the camera tagged along. We glassed some 40 different bulls on that hunt, and whether they had trophy horns or not, my duty was clear. I had to sneak up as close as my own buckling legs and the moose themselves would allow, mount the camera on its tripod and start shooting film. By the time that hunt came to an end, I didn't give a sneeze whether I ever saw a moose again, much less a movie camera. Of course, I've seen plenty of both, because if you're in the guiding business you don't shake either moose or movie cameras that easily.

S eldom in the past 25 years has there been a fall morning when some otherwise sensible chap wasn't plaguing me with the following question: "Think we're going to connect with a bull today?"

How do I know whether he's going to connect with a bull or not? If I answer "Yes," we don't cut a hot track from dawn till dusk and the blame, of course, is mine. If I reply "No," we come face to face with a trophy bull half a mile out from camp. And the fellow goes happily home with a rack of horns he has no place to hang, 600 or 700 pounds of meat his wife doesn't want, plus the firm conviction that the guide who helped him get all this junk knows nothing at all about moose.

But the annual guiding season is only of brief duration for me, a month or six weeks in the fall. After the last hunting party trails south, surely it is the time when I can sit back, relax and let the rest of the moose go by. But that's not the way the moose have it figured. As if knowing that I've a poor appetite for their meat, within a day or two of my bidding farewell to those that have gone, the moose start crowding in on me. From north, south, east and west they come like a swarm of bees. And given a choice of the two, I reckon I'd settle for the bees. They, at least, make with honey while all I can expect of moose is Trouble.

It has always been a mystery to me why a bull moose that I'd have given an eyetooth to meet up with a few days ago, when a hunter was at my side almost busting for the chance of a shot, would, as soon as the hunter is gone, walk innocently up to my back door as if to say, "Am I the guy you've been looking for?"

In case some skeptical reader doubts this lament of mine, I'm accompanying the story with a few photos to back up my argument that I have just cause for grumbling. One three-year-old bull moose, which I encountered on a December afternoon while tending a line of mink traps, toted one of the most inhospitable set of eye guards on his horns that I've ever seen on any bull. They were almost 15 inches long and pointed like knitting needles. I'll remember those eye guards for many years to come. I was only five feet away from them when I stopped to size them up.

We collided by the shoreline of a large lake, the bull steering due south, I due north. We both dragged to a stop when only 20 yards separated us.

"Scat," I gently breathed, thinking maybe I could bluff him into a slight shift in course.

But that bull had a mind of his own. He planted both front feet solidly down in the snow, dropped his left ear, ruffed his mane and glared at me. Then he belched, and it wasn't a polite belch either. Being slightly familiar with moose talk, I decoded that belch as meaning, "Better get scatting yourself."

"Then how about a nice friendly photo?" I argued, breaking my 35-mm camera from its case and nervously adjusting the lense opening. The bull cleared his nostrils, lowered those lethal eye guards and closed the distance between us to five forlorn feet.

"Hold it a minute," I stuttered, forcing my heart back down my gullet and wondering where my brains were. Hold it he did, looking me squarely in the eye, shaking his head slightly as if to make good and sure that both eye guards got into the picture.

If he'd lowered those eye guards and lunged forward five feet? Let's not go into such nasty imponderables. Fact is, after treating me to 30 seconds of disdainful appraisal, he made a 90° turn and headed for a nearby willow thicket.

Having maneuvered myself clear of that deal with ribs intact, surely I had a right to expect that I could snowshoe on home without bumping into further hair-raising situations. But no, I'm not that lucky. Just as I was about to step off the ice onto snow-covered land, what do I see lying squarely in the middle of the trail? Sure enough, moose. Two cows and a bull.

"Shucks, don't pay any attention to me," I grunted as my camera again moved into action. "Hog the whole trail if you like, I can always go around." Hog that trail they did, making me go cautiously around them.

I've heard it said that any man's home is his castle. Not mine. If I stroll to the sitting-room window on a bright sunny morning and gaze out on what should be a peaceful scene, what do I see cluttering things up a few feet from the glass? You're right. I can't even visit the backhouse—no indoor plumbing within 100 miles of us—without often having to sit there on a frosty seat wondering if there will be a moose parked on the trail when I try to get back to the house. Sure enough, there is. And while my common sense suggests that I tote my old .303 Ross rifle along whenever nature calls, and line its grimy barrel on any confounded moose between me and the outhouse, I'm so sick of moose that I hate going to the trouble of squeezing the trigger. Apart from that, who wants a dead moose blocking the path when you've urgent business outdoors? So instead of pointing a rifle barrel, I point my finger and argue, "You and I have a few million acres of parking space around here. Will you kindly get off that trail and go squat elsewhere?"

And, occasionally, they gang up on me. One moose interfering with the right of way can sometimes mean a peck of trouble, but one I don't mind. I'll even allow that maybe any healthy man of the woods should be able to bluff his way past two moose. But when four stand there, refusing to budge an inch, I begin to think that maybe it's time

I quit these woods for keeps and give them back to the moose.

It's almost light-the-lamp time, and since dawn I've coaxed my snowshoes along a line of traps. There's a fair load of fur on my packboard, the snowshoes are about out of gas and my belly is so empty it's saying hullo to my backbone. All I want right now is to get through to the house, slip the pack, dump down on a chair and fortify myself with a stiff slug of home brew. Yet, here I must stand fruitlessly arguing with four moose, trying to get them off the packed snow of the trail so I can stay on it myself. As usual, it's the moose that keep the trail and I who must swing aside and break virgin snow to pass them.

Most anyone else can at least sleep on his troubles and forget them until morning. Not me. No sooner do I park an ear on the pillow and doze off, dreaming of some land of milk and honey that's never seen a moose track, than I am jarred back to reality by my wife's elbow gouging me in the ribs.

"Wake up, Eric, and see what all that noise is about at the back door." I have a good idea what the racket is even before my eyes unglue.

"They're feuding again," I groan. Whenever two moose have a grudge to settle, where do they come to settle it? Our back door, of course. And if I step out to referee the bout and see them break clean in the clinches? They quit feuding with one another and start feuding with me.

During the winter months, our neighbors—anyone living within a 30-mile radius—avoid our home at Meldrum Lake. About three years ago, my wife's cousin Jennie decided she'd like to spend a winter with us, and we told her come right along. She didn't stay long. When stepping from the outhouse one bright crisp morning, she spied a cow and a calf moose flanking the path, the cow a few feet from the right of it, the calf an equal distance to the left. Now Jennie was born and raised right here in these Chilcotin sticks, and she knows a thing or two about moose. At most any other time of year, she would have discreetly reentered the place and stayed there until the cow and calf had gone. But there's neither cheer nor warmth, or much of anything else in any outdoor facility when the mercury is at 25 below, so Jennie decided to make a sprint for the house. That was a slight mistake in tactics, for any well-bred cow moose gets peeved when anything gets between her and her calf. But Jennie had to do just that to regain the warmth of the house.

I was sitting at the kitchen table drinking a cup of coffee when I heard the racket. Half human, half screech owl, that's how it sounded to me. Having some idea of what it might be all about, I lunged for the door and jumped out on the porch. I got there just in time to grab Jennie by the seat of her overalls, toss her into the kitchen and bang the door shut on the nose of the disgruntled cow.

That ended Jennie's visit. "You and your darned moose," she pouted later, swinging aboard her pony and heading for more hospitable pastures.

You can't have friends and moose too. One late November afternoon, a cattle rancher whose spread lies 25 miles downcreek from my cabin pulled his pinto to a stop at our door. He was hunting some missing yearling steers that had summer-ranged west of our beaver dams.

"Stick your horse in the barn and bunk here overnight," I invited.

"Don't mind if I do," he replied, coming out of the saddle. He had a large collie dog with him that looked part timber wolf to me. Seeing me eye the dog, he said, "Best cow dog in the Chilcotin. Yes sir, when Chummy starts after an animal, something just naturally has to move."

"You'd better shut Chummy in the barn with your horse," I said thoughtfully, my eyes still on the dog.

Next morning, just after daylight, we went to the barn, and while I forked hay into the manger the rancher watered his horse. We were halfway back to the house, coming through a scatter of cottonwoods, when I jerked to a halt. A few yards ahead of me, just emerging from a thicket of willows, was a cow moose with twin calves trailing behind her. I recognized that cow right away and sucked air down into my lungs. "The heavyweight champ of Meldrum Lake herself," I breathed uneasily.

The old cow had taken the title sometime back in 1945 when she'd whipped the stuffing out of a bull that was as punch drunk as he was big. Since then I'd seen her defend the title a dozen or more times and lick all contenders. She was dynamite, that old cow, just waiting for something or somebody to touch a flame to her fuse. At the sight of the old reprobate, I made a swift mental calculation. We were about 80 yards from the back porch. Though the trail itself was well packed, over 18 inches of loose snow was on either side of it.

And the old cow, moving in on the trail between us and the house, hated the scent of strangers as a grizzly hates wolverine scent.

"Stay put right here," I instructed the rancher. "I'll move up the trail and try to herd that moose back into the willows. Then you can make a break for the house."

But I'd forgotten about Chummy. The dog had sneaked out of the barn and was now trailing along at his master's heels. But I wasn't aware of that when I started toward the moose.

Hefting a sizable pole, I moved cautiously up the path. The two calves were just stepping away from the brush and the cow was 10 feet from the trail when I drew parallel to her. "Get back into that brush," I politely pleaded. "Can't a guy have visitors without—" The words jammed in my throat. A sudden yip from the dog warned me of mortal danger. I heard the rancher shout, "Chummy, come to heel." But Chummy had other heels in mind. He came loping up the trail, aiming for the cow.

Save himself who can! Out of the corner of one eye I saw the cow's ears flatten. From the corner of the other eye I saw her mane stand on end. That was all I waited to see. I suddenly recollected that I had pressing business at the house.

I heard a squeal from the dog as the cow bore down on him. My eyes fixed on the five-foot wire fence enclosing my wife's flower garden. The trail passed within four feet of the fence. Chummy was racing along at my heels, and I could almost feel the hot breath of the cow at the nape of my neck as I neared the fence. I could also hear the swish of air as her front hoofs flicked out at Chummy. I flung myself over the fence, clearing its top wire by almost six inches. Then I went to digging snow.

The dog was howling like a coyote with its feet in a trap as he circled the house and started back down the trail toward his master. I cautiously hefted up from the snow to see the cattleman flying through air, aiming for a snow-laden brush pile 15 feet off the trail. Chummy and the moose were almost alongside him when he hit that pile and ducked into a hole. Never in the long history of brush piles has so much flesh and bone managed to crowd itself into so small a hole.

But Chummy knew of a better one. He lined for the barn and the small window at the back that hadn't been closed after I'd shoveled out the manure. The cow plastered his rear end with a left as he hefted up from the manure pile and hit the same mark again as he

i can't even sit by my back door to hatch a story about some hunt without a bunch of moose sticking their noses into the plot.

hurled through the hole. After sticking her head inside to make sure the dog wouldn't be leaving his corner for the next several minutes, the cow shook herself and trotted off to round up the family.

After settling the nerves in his stomach with three fried eggs, four rashers of bacon, 10 hotcakes and four cups of coffee, the cattleman got his horse from the barn and took off down the trail. "Be sure and drop in on us again," I sang out in farewell. He has never been back.

Now maybe you'll think I'm romancing, but it's the truth that we don't dare leave the back door open for fear a moose will barge into the kitchen and flop down at the table. I can't even sit down on a block of wood outside the cabin on a wintry afternoon and hatch out a story of some hunt without a bunch of moose coming along to stick their big ugly noses into the plot. Only just the other day I was—

Excuse me, but that's my wife shouting at me from the backyard and, women being what they are, I'd better pay heed. "The clothes-line?" I shout back. "What about it? I helped you hang out the wash, didn't I? You say there's a bull moose out there pawing the clothes? He's going hell-for-leather through the woods with your brassiere at half-mast on his horn? So what am I supposed to do about it? Get the Royal Mounted Police and charge him with indecent exposure?" Oh me, I'm plumb sick of moose.

❖ ❖ ❖ ❖ ❖ ❖ ❖ ❖ ❖ ❖ ❖ ❖ ❖

taLL
BUT SHORT

I hear you're a mighty good hand at taxidermin', so I brung you this here mountain lion to stuff. Was I out huntin'? No sir, that lion was a pet that I raised sence it was a pup. Why shore, I shot it. Tell you why.

Toby was a mighty tame lion for a long while. But one day I came home and Toby wasn't hungry for his vittles. And there wasn't a hen left in the henhouse. I almost shot Toby then and there, but I figgered the hens wasn't layin' nohow, so I let it pass.

A while after, I came home one day and again Toby wasn't hungry. This time the goat was missin'. Well, she'd dried up anyway, so I let the matter pass.

Now, I had some of my family livin' with me—Uncle Horace and Cousin Herb. Well sir, one day Uncle Horace disappeared, and that lion looked mighty happy and contented. Now, Uncle Horace was a real old gaffer, and he'd been around a lot and had had a good time, so I fetched the lion a good kick in the ribs and let it go at that.

A month afterward, Cousin Herb turned up missin', and the lion was spittin' buttons. I allow you I laid into that cat till he howled. I thought I really learned him a lesson.

Well, wet my powder if I didn't come home one day and find that lion purrin' like a coffee grinder and my hound dog, Scatter, gone.

Well sir, that was too much. I grabbed my rifle and gave that cussed, double-crossin', confounded old lion a ball right through the lights.

And there he is. Stuff 'im up and fix 'im pretty, will ye? After all, he's my whole blessed family.

Elizabeth Schmitz

the air around my catfish filled with irate bees, and the
seat of my pants fairly caught fire.

Honey the Hard Way

by Ed Mason

THE VINEGAR-JUG CORK MADE A couple of businesslike dips. As the ripples widened across the still pool under the big maple, I grasped my hickory pole with both hands and dug my bare toes into the mud. The cork bobbed again and started nodding across the water in a steady pull.

I gave a mighty heave. The hickory bent, stood arched for a brief moment, then sent a big, yellow-bellied catfish whishing up into the branches of the maple to land against the trunk with a slimy thump. There he lodged. The line was tangled in twigs and bark. There was much tail-flapping and fluttering of leaves.

Dropping the pole, I scrambled up the tree to dislodge my fish. Halfway up I became conscious of a loud and angry buzzing.

The sound didn't register until a wicked whine zoomed past my ear. Something made a suicide dive into my hair and lashed down at my scalp with a hot little needle of fire. There was another buzz, followed by a stab on my cheek. I shot a glance upward and saw the air around my catfish filled with irate bees, pouring from a hole not far from his flapping tail. About that time the seat of my pants fairly caught fire.

The decision was instinctive. I jumped. The cool waters of the creek cut out the savage drone of a thousand warriors and let me concentrate on certain specific areas of my anatomy that seemed to be getting tighter and hotter by the moment.

Only one thing was certain. I'd found a bee tree—the hard way! I was whimpering with pain and grieving the loss of my fine, fat yellowbelly, yet a little surge of elation swept through me.

I'd heard Granddad, Dad, my uncles and the neighbors casually mention finding such a treasure trove and had once been present on a sharp autumn day when a snaggly elm fell before the axes. There'd been honey, a tubful of it, golden and drippy; much laughter, joshing, and yells when someone got stung. Since that day I'd craned my neck till it was stiff, trying to discover a "whopping big swarm" in every likely-looking tree along the creek. Now I'd found one.

If you've never found a bee tree and helped to cut it, you've missed part of living. Hunting wild bees is emotionally akin to looking for gold. Once it gets in your blood, you're like a sheep-killing dog—after it until the end.

The tree is generally discovered by accident or by a diligent search in the summer, when the workers are active and create noise enough around their home to attract attention. Experts resort to the use of a bee box and bee-lining. When the find is made it's a bonus in outdoor living. There's a mental mapping of location and a long wait till the bees have finished their work and the weather is chilly enough to render them only mildly dangerous.

During this period you have time to see the neighbor or acquaintance who owns the land and find out whether he's willing to have the tree cut—and, of course, be in on the fun. A fishing trip or squirrel hunt past the place can reveal whether cutting the tree will destroy a valuable coon or squirrel den. In many cases you need saw off only the actual limb where the bees are, leaving the rest of the tree intact.

Some Come to Kibitz

Even if you are one who cringes at the very mention of bees, a poor soul who swells up like a poisoned pup from the lash of a single stinger, don't be too sure you wouldn't enjoy cutting a bee tree. I have a friend who will just about break out in welts if he passes strained honey in a grocery store, yet he's nuts about bee trees. He doesn't stay close when the tree is ready to fall. Neither does he help "ladle 'er out of the hole." He stands back at a safe distance, alternately shouting instructions, guessing the size of the take and trembling in terror. Of course he's usually the first man in the party to get socked. But just mention a bee tree and he wants to know when you'll cut it.

Like the gambler who remembers only those times when luck was riding high, the bee-tree addict recalls most easily the occasions that yielded lots of honey along with the fun. Those are the ones he'll tell you about when he reminisces. The amount of booty, however, generally has little to do with the actual humor connected with this warped sense of adventure.

Cousin Nick and I left a duck blind on a hot fall morning and gave up hunting as a bad job. On the way home we forded the creek, where a sizeable ash hung over the bank. It was a bee tree we'd known about for months. It had been on the agenda for this weekend. Mother had emphatically vetoed the idea. Her beloved son would be half of a high-school debate team on Monday. Knowing the ways of boys—and men, for that matter—with bee trees, she ruled it an inopportune time to flirt with bumps and swellings around the face and head.

This ultimatum went through our minds as we looked up at the slick bee hole, where a few lazy workers droned about, sunning themselves.

It was my fault we couldn't cut the tree. I felt guilty. Nick was older, had shed such foolish activities as school, debating classes and other afflictions of youth. He had a job. Monday he'd have to go after the fall plowing. A couple of stingers meant little to him. Probably a big flight of ducks would be on next weekend, anyhow.

We went home for dinner. Thus fortified, we caught up the guns and detoured by the barn where the axes and crosscut saws were kept. With the guns stacked in the corncrib in exchange for a galvanized bushel basket, we were off, disobedient but at a fast trot.

Peeled down to shirtsleeves under the ash, we fell to work. It was evident the tree would fall to span the little river from bank to bank. Just before she toppled Nick had a pang of conscience. "Maybe you better stay back and let me take it from here," he cautioned. "If you get stung in the face, there'll be the devil to pay."

It was only a gesture on his part, and he knew it. Instead I volunteered, once the tree fell, to run out on the log and stuff the hole with a couple of cotton flannel mittens, then take my chances with the few sentinels already in the air around the hole. This was flimsy planning, since you can't get honey out of a tree without cutting the thing open.

Up above, the warm sun plus the jar of axes on the trunk had produced quite a cloud of bees. They looked a little dopey but definitely on the prod.

Nick hit a final lick with the ax. The tree toppled. Its top crashed with a bounce on the far bank of the stream. I was across the log like a cat, the wad of mittens in my hand. The bee hole was about over midstream. One stride from it I met head-on a little jet demon who was really on the beam. He hit me just under the right eye and socked in his dagger up to the hilt. The shock fairly knocked me backward off the log, and there I stood up to my armpits in November creek water.

An Irresistible Target

My husky cousin charged out on the tree trunk and flopped crosswise over the log to extend me a helping hand. In so doing his muscular and somewhat ample fanny was pointed at the treetop. Up there half a hundred thoroughly aroused insects had been diving in circles, looking for their home, for the last 30 seconds. Who could resist such a target, including a mad bee?

I felt rather than heard the pair of words Nick uttered a few inches above my face. We went to the bank, he by wood and I by water. The time was nothing flat.

every HANδfuL of HONey meant a stinger, every stinger meant a swig.

Did you ever try making a serious point in debate before an audience of your peers with one eye swollen completely shut and half your mouth so thick the only way to get a sound out was to pucker up the good side to meet it until you looked like a stranded sucker in a mud hole? But I guess it's no worse, at that, than riding a plow seat all day long with a lump, egg size and sore as a boil, located precisely at the point of friction.

That experience should have cured us then and there, but we went back a few days later, only to cuss the coon who'd had sense enough to wait for a cold snap before robbing the robbers.

Another time some gentlemen of our acquaintance found a bee tree while fishing on Lotts Creek in our home county. During the summer they got permission, gathered a few select recruits and set the appointed day.

It was Sunday. The day was ideal, with snappy weather, but not bitter cold. Since it was a congenial crowd, each member had thought of the welfare of his buddies, putting in his pocket a little something to take the bite out of the air. It was a long walk to the tree, and spirits were passed around throughout the journey. When the party reached the bee tree, all the buzz wasn't inside it.

In the next half hour more bottles were handled than axes. When the crew finally beavered off the stump, there was a resounding crack of splintered wood. The whole trunk split wide open.

If ever wild-bee hunters struck a bonanza, this was it. The old shell was full of honey. With lusty yells, half a dozen tipsy and even benumbed gents dashed forward with tubs and pails to scoop up the prize. The bees in their protected hollow, numb but not dormant, arose in threes and sixes and went to work.

Every handful of honey meant a stinger. Every stinger meant a swig. The tree was full of honey, but the supply of anesthetic was ample to see the party through. The ensuing hour mashed hazel brush down over half an acre, filled all the tubs with honey and chips, emptied all the bottles and left countless stingerless bees buzzing feebly in the drippings of their own ravaged storehouse. Seldom has the eye of man seen a stickier, more wobbly or more swollen caravan than the one that finally staggered back up Lotts Creek bottom.

A drippy jalopy stopped by our house just before sunset. It disgorged three unrecognizable citizens bearing a tub of honey, twigs and bark. Knobby welts puffed their faces and hands. They talked with an alcoholic thickness enhanced to gibberish by the wild-bee venom in their swollen lips.

No pity could have subdued the laughter we pealed into the chill evening. In disgust they climbed aboard their crate and went chugging off.

Grandfather, a veteran wild-bee hunter and a keeper of tame bees, emerged from around the house as the three got under way. He'd missed the sight and I was in no condition to talk. He saw the honey tub at the front gate. With a professional gesture he dipped a finger into the golden stuff and licked. The smile that came over his face was almost ethereal.

"Stop 'em! Stop 'em!" he shouted. "Find out where that tree is," he thundered. "I'll give 20 bucks for the queen to this hive!"

Instead I dipped my finger into the tub of honey and sampled. The stuff was half bourbon!

I've been in on quite a few bee-tree cuttings, and somebody invariably pays. If it's too warm, you know the chances are against you. If it's too cold, you get careless and sit or put your hand on a bee, who saves his last breath to power the stinger. Even the ultra-innocent bystander often gets tagged.

Disregarding property rights as well as conservation practices, a couple of professional poachers decided to steal a bee tree from a big and rugged Missouri farmer known for his extreme good nature and easygoing ways.

On Sunday just before church time, they parked down the road till his car pulled out. Certain he'd be in the regular family pew, they sneaked through the fence and fell to work in a frenzy of basswood chips.

The farmer, however, had remained behind to repair the corn picker. The sound of chopping down by his line fence on the branch seemed to indicate that his neighbor had chosen this time to fix the water gap left by fall rains. So he left his work of the moment to go and help. He was a devout man, but liked a mess of squirrel. Along with the hammer and staples, he carried the old double-gun. It was an opportunity to get in a shot on Sunday without setting a bad example for the kids.

While still some distance from the choppers he perceived that neither was his neighbor and that they weren't working at the water gap. Curious, he approached through a convenient corn patch to look the situation over. The tree under attack was his favorite squirrel den. He'd never noticed the bees, but a few minutes of watching revealed the situation and the identity of his uninvited guests.

His first impulse was to dash up and boot the two bums over the fence. But he wasn't that kind of a fellow. The tree was cut half through anyway, so it would fall in the next stiff wind.

He just waited, and as he did a slow burn came over this good-natured son of the soil who'd give you the shirt off his back if you needed it. But indecision was still mixed with his mounting anger.

With furtive glances in all directions, the choppers worked up quite a lather before the tree fell. Expertly they notched out a six-foot section and pried it open.

Lifting out a fat length of honeycomb, one of the thieves remarked on the future emotions of the owner when he discovered their work. Included in this phrase was a reference to the farmer's ancestry, plus some derogatory stuff about church-going. All this was audible in the nearby corn patch. A decision was made.

It took the robbers several minutes to clean out the hollow and place the honey carefully in a tub, taking a few stingers in the process. When the job was done, they picked up the tub between them and started to beat it. The cornstalks rattled with the charge of a big man moving fast. One of the trespassers later confessed that the barrels of the old 12 gauge looked as big as sewer pipes. Orders were brief and direct. The poachers carried the tub of honey up the long hill to the house, set it in the yard and got helped into the road in a most effective manner.

Our friend was sitting on the porch beside his tub of loot when the family came home from church. But all was not milk and honey as he had expected. Knowing the good nature of her big, friendly husband, his wife refused to believe his story. To this day she accuses him of staying home from church to cut a bee tree.

CONTENTS NOTED - Returning to retrieve his lunch and thermos of coffee he had stashed in a tree crotch, a Jamestown hunter found only this note: "Thanks for the coffee and peanut-butter sandwiches. Next time bring some honey." It was signed, "Your Woodland Friend, Yogi Bear."
- Neil Chaffee, DUNKIRK-FREDONIA (NY) EVENING OBSERVER.

DRY RUN - We like the story of the Iowa fisherman who, hoping to change his luck, followed a hatchery truck leaving the federal trout hatchery east of Manchester through three towns to the airport at Waterloo, where the fish were loaded onto a Navy transport plane. - Bill Severin, WATERLOO (IA) COURIER.

IGNORANT BLISS - Cap Harrison used to say that the reason so many beginning trapshooters hit so many targets at first is that "they haven't yet found out how hard they are to hit."
- Outdoor Roundup With Casey, PROVO (UT) HERALD.

STOOL PIGEON - After several friends reported seeing a buck deer with a red camp stool on its antlers, Neil Bailey, who lost the stool while hunting, advertised for its return and got it back from Burnett Otterson, who shot the buck, still carrying the stool, 20 miles away. - EAU CLAIRE (WI) LEADER.

out popped the cartridges, one by one.

By the time i got off a shot, the crazy ram was up the mountain.

i was quivering hard when i snook up behind the anthill.

set-up shots give Lots of good gunners the willies, worries 'em.

panicked, the grizzly hit the tree so hard it broke off with a Large crack.

BUCK FEVER and How to Cure It

by Jack O'Connor

NO ONE WHO REALLY ENJOYS HUNTING is COMPLETELY FREE FROM IT.

THE WORST CASE OF BUCK FEVER I've ever had was not buck fever at all but ram fever. It hit me years ago in the Mexican state of Sonora—and when it hit, it really laid me low.

I'd crawled off my cot an hour or so before, and my Mexican compadre and I had eaten breakfast in the predawn darkness. It was just getting light when, glum and half asleep, I sat beside the Mexican as he drove an ancient Model-T Ford along a dim road that skirted a ragged mountain. The plan was for him to leave me at one end of the mountain, then I'd work back along the crest to camp, hunting sheep on the way. It would be 10 miles of rough going.

At that time I'd never shot a sheep and consequently I knew all about sheep hunting. The notion that I might run into a ram right on a desert flat would have seemed as preposterous as encountering an alligator. I hadn't even loaded the Springfield sporter I had with me in a sheepskin case.

Suddenly the Mexican slammed on the brakes and yelled in Spanish, "Look at the big ram!"

About 20 feet from the car and crossing the road was an old desert bighorn with a fine, rugged head. I fell out of the car, fumbling with the buckles of that miserable case, trembling, sweating, tearing off my fingernails. I finally got the rifle out, then tried to load it. After

I'd dropped a couple of cartridges on the ground, I managed to get one in the magazine. Should I shoot now or should I put in another cartridge in case I missed? I decided to make doubly sure and put in three. Then I noticed the front sight cover was still on. I cut my right hand taking the cover off. By now the ram had run nearly 200 yards and was about to get into brush at the base of the mountain. I threw my madly wavering rifle to my shoulder, fired one shot that must have missed the animal by 40 feet. Then my trembling legs would support me no longer. I sat down quivering beside the road. This was too much for the Mexican. He started to giggle.

"Shut up, you cabrón," I told him. "If you laugh anymore, I'll shoot you—and because you aren't a sheep I won't miss."

I've had buck fever many times in varying degrees of intensity, but that attack was the worst. It was months before I could laugh about it.

It's a great deal easier to find something funny in someone else's buck fever than in your own. It's pretty comical—when it happens to the other guy. Here's a story on a pal:

Back in the days of plentiful deer and large trophy bucks in Arizona's Kaibab forest, my amigo and I had just come over a ridge so that we could look into a sparsely timbered draw when a beautiful big buck came out. He was only about 200 yards away, and for at least 300 yards he trotted along at right angles to us, looking like the prettiest storybook deer you ever dreamed about. My pal was a good shot and a good hunter, but for some reason this wasn't his day. He went completely to pieces. Instead of sitting down and taking his time, he began blazing away offhand. His bullets hit above, below, under and in front of the deer. Finally the buck ran around a point and out of sight. Apparently my friend thought an explanation was in order. He turned to me, trembling, his eyes glazed, sweat beading his brow. "I was j-j-just t-t-trying to t-t-turn him," he said.

It's a universal ailment among hunters, this buck fever. Most of the time it's simply funny, but it can also be tragic. In the spring of 1956 two Alaskan hunters were killed by the same grizzly. Many theories have been advanced to explain how one bear could kill two armed men. It occurs to me that they could simply have been paralyzed by buck fever.

Not long before I hunted tiger in 1955, an Indian sportsman from

New Delhi was killed by one of the big cats in an area where I hunted. He'd wounded the tiger from a machan. The cat didn't go far before it lay down in a brush patch. When it was beaten out it came right at the hunter across 50 yards of open ground. The sportsman never even raised his double .450/400 to his shoulder. Instead he stood paralyzed as the enraged beast came swiftly on. The tiger killed him.

Experienced hunters aren't supposed to get buck fever, but I've seen many an old-timer with the shakes. Often a new species will bring it on. Pronghorn antelope seem to be particularly bad at this. Some years ago I went on an antelope hunt with a friend who was a crack shot and who had killed dozens of deer and elk. That first morning he missed at least 10 antelope at ranges where he would ordinarily kill a woodchuck. He blamed his poor shooting on the wind, the light, finally on the fact that his rifle must certainly have changed point of impact. Meantime, I'd shot an antelope, so after we had eaten lunch my friend borrowed my rifle. By that time he'd calmed down somewhat and he got his antelope. "I told you that rifle of mine was off," he said. But not long after that I killed a sitting jackrabbit with his rifle at 200 yards. There was nothing wrong with it.

Another time when a friend and I were hunting antelope we came over a rise and saw a bunch of six does and one respectable buck coming in to water. I cautioned my friend to wait until the buck came up over the bank in plain sight. But the moment the buck's head came over the bank he shot and missed. The buck ran out from behind the bank and stopped. My friend missed three more times. The buck then ran up on a hillside about 175 yards away and stopped once more. My pal reloaded and opened a barrage. "You're shooting high," I told him. "Of course," he snarled. "That buck's 500 yards away." We can laugh over it now, but he still has no recollection of those close-range shots at the buck in the open.

A Yukon guide told me about a client of his, a good shot and an experienced hunter, who came unexpectedly on a wonderful white ram. He sat down carefully and, without firing a shot, ejected every cartridge in his .300 Magnum. The ram was only about 75 yards away, so the guide knocked it over. The hunter delightedly rushed toward it, and the guide, a tactful fellow, quietly picked up his client's unfired cartridges and put them in his pocket. The hunter was shocked and disappointed to find that there was but one bullet hole in the ram, and to this day he hasn't the faintest idea that he never pulled the trigger of his rifle.

What a good case of buck fever can do to the imagination of an ordinarily sensible taxpayer must be seen to be believed. I once was hunting with an excitable friend in an area where the shooting of does was prohibited. Presently we came upon a little yearling doe below us about 100 yards away in a basin. My companion began to sweat and shake and threw up his rifle.

"Don't shoot," I said. "That's a doe."

"Keep away from me, you idiot," he hissed. "That's the biggest buck I've ever seen." He touched off his shot as the sights wavered past the doe, and down it went. He was flabbergasted when he couldn't find antlers.

I don't think it's any disgrace to get buck fever, as those who suffer most from it are imaginative, high-strung and often gifted people for whom the world is full of wonders. I don't think anyone who genuinely enjoys hunting is ever completely free from it. The man who doesn't get excited by hunting doesn't enjoy it. Some of the buckiest characters I've ever known were also the most experienced.

One of these is a man who has specialized in guiding antelope hunters for many years and who lives right in antelope country. You would think that if anyone would be immune to antelope fever, it would be this man. But he isn't. Whenever he sees a good antelope trophy within range of one of his dudes he comes untied.

Like any form of nervousness, buck fever's catching, and it takes a dude with a will of iron to keep calm when his guide is boiling over. A tape recording of his instructions to a hunter would sound like this: "Look at that buck—third from the right. The one with its head down. Now he's got his head up. Now he's the second from the right. What a head! You'll never see another like it. Now, don't get excited. Don't shake. Don't jerk the trigger. Shoot before that damned doe walks in front of him!" About that time the hunter, no matter how experienced, generally closes his eyes, screams and jerks the trigger.

Another guide I know, a man of considerable fame, gets buck fever so badly when he has a client out that he seldom guides anymore. Instead he stays in camp, cooks, skins out trophies and wrangles horses. The more he guided, the more excited and buck-feverish he got, and the more he affected his customers. Once when an excited dude missed a big bull moose at less than 100 yards, he became so unhinged that he hauled off and booted the dude right where he sat down. He immediately apologized, but the incident didn't tend to promote harmony and good client relations. Now that he's quit guiding, his ulcers don't bother him so much.

The old belief is that buck fever is like whooping cough—once you've had it you're forever immune. But as we have seen, this isn't necessarily so. Our two guides were men of vast experience, but they were buck-fever-prone, just as some people are accident-prone. I feel sorry for hunters who are made helpless by buck fever, but I feel sorrier for those who never have it.

The keener the hunter is over a certain animal, the more likely he is to get the shakes. I'll never forget my first black bear. I was pussy-footing along in one of those beautiful Arizona forests of yellow pine, Gambel's oak and alligator juniper, with occasional groves of piñon on the south slopes. This was mule deer and turkey country. There were a few elk in those days, and black-bear sign was fairly plentiful. But it was almost unheard of to run into a bear that hadn't been put up by dogs.

Then I actually *did* see a black bear. Shining like a newly polished shoe in the early morning sun, he was rooting around for piñon nuts across a shallow draw about 150 yards away. I began to shake violently and uncontrollably. I put my rifle to my shoulder, tried to line up the sights offhand. I couldn't do it. I sat down, but I was shaking so badly I think I would have missed an elephant. I crawled over to a log, took a deep breath and tried to relax. All this time the bear was feeding busily. For a minute or so my shakes continued, but the long rest steadied my nerves as well as my muscles. Presently I could see the gold front bead against the glossy black of the bear's shoulder. My temperature and respiration got back to something like normal, and when I squeezed the trigger the bear fell on his nose and never moved. The 150-gr. .30/06 bullet had been placed exactly right.

It is good antibuck-fever medicine to be relatively indifferent as to whether you get a trophy or not. That's one reason, I believe, why women are so often good big-game shots. My wife can take big-game hunting or leave it. She goes along with me for the ride. Never have I seen her have the slightest trace of buck fever when she was after deer, antelope, elk or javelina. The first deer she ever shot at was a tremendous buck with a superb trophy head. She put a little .25 Remington bullet right behind its shoulder, and down he came. Her first antelope, a beauty, flustered her not at all. We'd just begun to hunt when we saw a herd of antelope just under the skyline. It was still too dark to see heads, but I was trying to make them out with binoculars. It was a tough job, partly because I had a touch of the buck myself and my hands were shaking. Keeping calm and using her head on this, her first antelope, my wife dropped flat on the ground so she could see the heads against the silver of the dawn sky. She picked out the largest, held the post of the scope above the buck's shoulder, and pulled it down and fired when the post disappeared into the antelope's black silhouette. I heard the crack of the rifle, dimly saw one of the whitish animals drop. The horns were massive, beautifully formed and just under 17 inches around the curve.

By this time you may think my wife's a pretty cool customer. She's never particularly cared if she shot any big game or not, but she's an ardent upland gunner. A cock pheasant roaring out from under her feet can make her jump a mile. The more seriously anyone takes an animal or bird, the more likely it is to make him jumpy. I don't suppose anyone gets jittery when he shoots a hog behind the ear for the fall butchering—but he doesn't get any kick out of it either.

Buck fever isn't very different from stage fright, if indeed it isn't the same thing. Some actors, I understand, never get stage fright, some get it now and then and others (some of the greatest) always get it. It's the same way with buck fever.

I suppose that if a psychiatrist went into the basic causes of this buck-fever business, he'd find that what lay behind it was a basic lack of self-confidence coupled with an overevaluation of the prize. The sheep hunter misses the easy shot at the big ram, the actor flubs his lines in a climactic scene, the tennis player serves a double fault at match point for the singles championship. All regard the prizes they seek very highly, but at the same time feel that they're probably not quite equal to the job.

The Canadian Indian who goes out to shoot a deer for stew meat, knowing that if he misses one he'll get a shot at another within 10 minutes, won't get buck fever. On the other hand, he might if he and his family were starving and if he had to take a difficult shot at the first deer he'd seen in two weeks. The sportsman who will knock over an ordinary buck without a quiver may possibly come apart at the seams when he runs into an especially fine head. Our hunter may also feel some sense of guilt for preparing to kill this animal he loves.

What can a hunter do about buck fever? Though experience may never make the jittery person completely immune, it helps. As a general thing, the man who has shot 15 deer is less prone to get the fever than the man who's shot none.

Another thing that helps is a lot of shooting practice, since, as we have seen, lack of self-confidence is one of the reasons for the ailment. The more anyone shoots, the more likely he is to do things right and automatically, even if he is surprised, startled and jumpy. The big buck may be running along the side of a hill, but if the hunter has shot hundreds of running jackrabbits, his rifle automatically swings along ahead of the buck and goes off at the right instant. A habit's a habit. On many occasions, I've seen experienced riflemen make good shots on game and then show all the signs of buck fever. One in particular hit a beautiful buck twice behind the shoulder at 250 yards, then got so shaky he had to rest for five minutes before his legs would support him.

Often a good but jittery hunter will do his stuff nicely if he has to react instantly, but flub easy shots if given time to think things over. I've seen many upland gunners who shoot well if a bird comes out without warning, but who simply can't connect if a bird is right under a pointing dog's nose and they have time to get worried. Other types shoot well if alone, but are so afraid they'll make themselves ridiculous that they never do well with an audience.

If a hunter finds himself getting spooky when the big chance presents itself, he should take the steadiest position possible, for there's nothing that will calm him down quicker than seeing his sights steady on the target. While I was sneaking up under cover of an anthill to take a crack at a beautiful African lion with a big blond mane, I was quivering like a debutante at her first ball. When I stuck my head around the anthill, the lion was still there, standing up in the high grass like a big dog and looking proud. I rested the .375 Magnum across the anthill and the picture of crosswires steady against the lion's neck calmed me down like a shot of tranquilizing drug. I squeezed the trigger as gently as if I'd been shooting from a bench rest.

If the hunter can remember to make himself relax, he'll find that buck fever has lost its bite. In an interview after the last World Series baseball game, a victorious pitcher said that in the clutch he took special pains to let all his muscles go loose for a moment and to breathe deeply between pitches. Tension is generally the villain in all kinds of poor shooting. It makes the skeet or trapshooter stop his swing, the upland gunner slow his muzzle and miss. It also makes the rifleman fight his rifle and try to hold it still by strength and awkwardness, with resultant tremor and trigger yanking. The good shot is the relaxed shot.

The buck-fever story to end buck-fever stories is one I heard years ago from Roy Hargreaves, famous Alberta and British Columbia outfitter. The tale is in my book, *Hunting in the Rockies*, and I related it once in an issue of *Outdoor Life*.

Roy had left a hunter sitting on a log right at timberline while he went off to glass a canyon. The dude was on one side of an open meadow and on the other a trail came out of the scattered timber about 100 yards away. The dude was enjoying the view when an enormous grizzly walked out of the trees and continued along the trail toward the dude. Startled half out of his wits, the hunter grabbed his rifle, threw a hasty shot at the bear and missed. The frightened bear whirled and headed back into the timber, but he ran into a tree, breaking it off short with a sharp crack.

Hearing what he thought were two shots, Roy ran back to the open park. He found that his dude had taken off in one direction and a big grizzly in another. When he found his client, the dude was pale, winded and his eyes were rolling wildly.

"Did you hit that grizzly?" Roy asked.

"N-n-no," he quavered, "I don't think so."

"You got two shots at him, didn't you?"

"N-no," said the dude, "I shot once and the bear shot once."

I was once so flustered by a grizzly that I wouldn't have been the least surprised if he'd whipped out a .38 Special and taken a shot at me. I know just how that guy felt.

taLL
BUT SHORT

Years ago, when I was guiding in British Columbia, I took out a party of three sports, and one of hem was a ventrilo—a ventriquo— one of those fellers that throws their voices and makes dummies talk. I knowed he was a ventrilo—I knowed he could do it, but the other fellers were strangers and they didn't know it, so I looked for some fun.

Well sir, we were out four days looking for bighorn sheep and we didn't find any, and everyone was disgusted, including me. Fourth night we were sitting in camp around a fire when a big gray wolf comes up to the edge of the clearing and squats there, looking at us. Then it pipes up and says, "What you fellers out for?"

Everybody looked dumbfounded, including the ventrilo—the guy that could throw his voice. But I was wise to his trick, so I says, "After sheep, bud. Bighorns. Got any dope on them?"

"Sure," says the wolf. "You passed up a good chance today. Tomorrow you backtrack for three, four miles till you come to that stand of blasted jackpine, then turn east and climb old Coffee Grinder Mountain. You'll find some good rams up there."

"Thanks," I says to the wolf. "We'll leave you a little mutton when we get finished."

So off goes the wolf. The sports acted like they were drunk or hearing things, but I kept a straight face.

Well, next day, still serious, I took them on the backtrack, and be durned if we didn't find good rams on the mountain!

Back in camp I called the ventrilo—the feller to one side and said, "I know you can throw your voice but how in Tophet did you know there were sheep up on that mountain?"

He gave me a kind of sick look and said, "Throw my voice? Say, when that wolf came up to camp last night I was so scared I was speechless!"

Jerry Ross

The Mad Trout and Other Rabid Game

by Charles Elliott

the mountaineer simply wasn't convinced that fish didn't have rabies like warm-blooded animals, so we agreed to carry the fish to the laboratory and have it positively tested for rabies.

WAS IN THE TENNESSEE MOUN-tains on a black bear hunt with hounds, which were used for bear hunting in that country. My hunting companion on this trip was from a large city nearby and I gathered from his remarks that he was not a hunter and had never shot a gun of any kind. He had an idea that killing a bear would increase his stature among his fellow humans.

He bought a 30-30 rifle and came to see me. I loaded the gun, explained all the safety devices and rules and let him shoot it. Since the guides had accepted him as my hunting partner, I considered it might be wise to stay close to him to keep him from shooting me or one of the guides or a dog. The thought occurred that normally I have more intelligence than to be caught in a situation of this kind.

We were near the crest of a ridge when the hounds struck a trail immediately below us. A guide close to the dogs yelled, "It's a black bear and he's coming straight toward you!"

The race got closer and louder and it sounded like the hounds were taking nips out of the bear's posterior with every jump. I was standing close enough to my hunting partner to keep him from shooting in the wrong direction, but with the race only a few yards away, I certainly did not anticipate his reaction. Apparently he lost his nerve completely. He actually screamed, threw down his rifle and shinnied up a tree so small that it bent under his weight.

The cub bear was not much bigger than the hound on its tail. As the race swept by, the tree bent under the weight of my hunting partner and he swung to the ground. He picked up his rifle and brushed it off with his sleeve. I knew he was embarrassed but he made no comment and neither did I.

Later, this hunting partner redeemed himself with a good shot in open woods. It got him a medium trophy bear that was, I am sure, the subject of more than one tall tale. My regret is that I could not be there to hear his daring exploits.

I am glad to brag that I considered myself a friend of Fred Bear, one of the most successful bow and arrow hunters in this modern world. His North American trophies with the broadhead included most of the big game animals and he added trophies listed as the most dangerous from other dark portions of the earth's surface.

Fred was with a friend on a picture-taking expedition in Alaska when they came unexpectedly, at rather close quarters, on an outsized bull moose. Fred feels certain they would have walked by without attracting undue attention, but his companion picked up a rock and threw it at the moose. The big animal whirled, saw the two men and charged.

Only one small tree grew near them on the tundra and Fred's longer legs got him to the tree steps ahead of his friend, who dived into a cavelike opening near the base of the tree. Fred had shinnied up the little sapling only inches higher than the moose could reach. The big bull, running full speed, hit the trunk of the small tree, almost breaking Fred's frantic handhold.

At this moment Fred's partner popped out of the cave. The moose left the tree and went after him for a short circle around the mouth of the cave. Just as the moose made another pass at the tree, Fred's partner again popped into the open.

"Stay in the cave!" Fred yelled.

"I can't!" his friend, three jumps ahead of the moose, yelled in reply. "I can't! There's a bear in there!"

I am sure there were no dramatics at the end of that experience because I can't remember exactly how it ended. I can only guess that the bear, annoyed by all the human commotion, happily escaped and the moose gave up and went on about its normal activities.

I am sure that our four-legged and our winged and other wild friends do not sit around trying to think of antics they might pull to amuse us as humans. All of their actions and reactions are completely natural. What we see in those actions as humor is the way we look at them from the human viewpoint.

In the high peaks of northern British Columbia I witnessed a scene to convince me that animals do have a definite sense of the comic. I was well camouflaged and elk hunting afoot and spending most of my time backed up against this tree or that one to study the timber ahead with my field glasses. I was hunting upwind, which gave me the distinct advantages of sight, sound and smell. I had been still for several minutes, studying the slope ahead, which was covered with a magnificent stand of fir and spruce timber.

I thought I was unobserved but a red squirrel passing overhead discovered me, came down to a lower limb and set up a chatter that I am sure was loaded with obscene language.

At almost the same time, two pine martins came within view. They were on a course that would have passed me by, but the scolding squirrel attracted their attention, so they turned and came directly toward my tree.

The squirrel didn't see the martins until they were directly below him at the tree trunk and were looking up at him. With what couldn't have been anything but a shriek of terror, the squirrel scampered up the tree trunk and took off at full speed through the crowns. The two pine martins stood on their hind legs and watched him go, then glanced at one another with what I am sure was amusement at the squirrel's alarm. They then turned and resumed their journey afoot through the woods. There was no question in my mind that they had enjoyed that little display as much as I did.

I have seen enough to convince me that animals have their own conception of what play is. Otters, mink and beaver entertain themselves by sliding down a muddy bank, splashing into the water, then swimming ashore to continuously repeat the performance. More than once have I seen young black bears climb a few feet up a tree trunk and jump off to take a rolling tumble on the ground. And I have seen young bears cuff one another and wrestle so hard and bite so viciously that they seemed to be in an actual fight. This is without question self-entertainment, which is every bit as obvious as children playing in the school yard.

fishing is a serious endeavor in which humor seldom finds a niche. But one vivid exception to this general statement might apply to my experience with the mad trout.

My mountain neighbor and friend, Pate Jones, had hooked a mammoth rainbow that he estimated was "a dam three feet long" and since he never used a net, he slid the fish ashore on a sandbar. His old hound ran down the bank and clamped its teeth on the hooked trout—something it had never done before. When Pate kicked the dog, the hook was jerked out of the trout's mouth. The rainbow flounced back into the river and swam away.

The next day the dog was slobbering and belligerent and the vet pronounced that it had rabies. Pate figured there was no way his dog could be thus afflicted except by biting the trout, which had to be sick with the distemper. In Pate's mind, all the trout in the river were suspect and dangerous. So he leaned his fishing rod in a corner of the cabin and resolved never to put another hook in the waters of Jacks River.

I told my friend and one of my angler partners, Dr. Tom Sellers, about Pate's experience with the rabid rainbow. Tom was director of the State Veterinary Department. He avowed, with a twinkle in his eye, that this was by all means well worth a scientific investigation.

We selected a bright day, with the barometer high, to make our bid for the huge trout. To test what and how the fish were hitting, we fished a section of the stream before we arrived at the bend where Pate had hooked the trout. Pate had refused to leave his plow and come with us, but when we arrived at what we knew as "The Glory Hole," Pate was there, sitting on a streamside boulder, with his fly rod propped up beside him.

"I got to figgerin,'" he said, "I ain't such a coward as to let you'uns git mad-trout bit on my account. So I come up to ketch that fish fer ye."

We tried, but there was no way of talking him into standing aside while we fished for the trout, so I suggested to Dr. Sellers, "Let him try. If he can't produce, we'll let the pool rest a while, then you can take over."

Reluctantly, Tom stepped back and Pate waded a few steps beyond the edge of the gravel bar and I'm sure that it was fear that caused his first poor cast. When no monster appeared to swallow him whole, he courageously took a few more steps to put him where he could flip his fly under the tree branches to a corner of the pool. The fly settled gently, swirled out of sight in an eddy and the line snapped taut.

There is hardly any way to describe those next few minutes. Pate let out a yell like a warring Cherokee and dived for the safety of the sandbar. In the mad scramble his foot slid off the wet face of a submerged river boulder. He went under, floundered out spluttering and plowed the remainder of the distance to the sandbar on his two knees and one hand. In some miraculous manner he held his rod tip up and kept a tight line.

Safely on the sand he stood up, streaming water, his rod in a dangerous arc. The pressure brought the trout, which looked as large as a Pacific salmon, out of the emerald depths. It somersaulted four feet into the air and fell back with a splash that wet the rock wall. Then the line, hissing audibly, cut downstream. The trout landed on its side and swept into the riffles, its broad tail flinging bright drops the width of the stream.

"Go with him!" I yelled.

Pate splashed across the shallow lower end of the bar, but the rainbow had righted itself and charged up the current, through the pool and over the granite ledge, throwing water like a stranded whale. Tom and I sprinted toward Pate, waving our nets like a couple of lacrosse players. Pate was screaming, "Stand back! Don't let that fish bite ya! Stan' back!"

The trout made another feeble jump, but its power was almost gone. Tom scooped his net under the fish and stumbled ashore, as carefully as if he were carrying the last vial of medicine to save all mankind.

He laid the trout out in the grass. Pate's hook was still in its jaw. Its gills were fiery red and the rainbow along its side was brilliant. With the mountain man's warning ringing in my ears, I slid the hook out. The fly was a Jock Scott, of the same pattern Pate had lost to him days before. Under Tom's steel tape, the rainbow measured 25 inches and was broad and heavy. Tom slowly closed one eye in my direction.

"Thank heaven," he said. "We caught him before he infected all the fish in north Georgia."

After a bit we tried to convince Pate that it was all a big laugh and that fish didn't have rabies like warm-blooded animals, but the mountaineer simply wasn't satisfied at our assurance, so we agreed to carry the fish to the laboratory and have it positively tested for rabies.

I have not yet been back to assure Pate that his rainbow had been given a clean bill of health. That information might be considered by some as favorable news. My thought was that any creek or river inhabited by wild rabid rainbow trout should be the most sumptuous fishing waters on earth.

The Argentine Way

by Eugene E. Wilson

WITH GAUCHOS GALLOPING FURIOUSLY BEHIND US, WE ROARED OUT ONTO THE PAMPAS ON A DUCK HUNT THAT RESEMBLED MOB WARFARE.

Luro deliberately swerved the big car into the pond. Staggering to our feet, we fired as the car raced on.

MAT STROTHER AND I CRAWLED on our bellies through the thin, parched grass of the Argentine pampas with the sun fairly frying our backs through our heavy shooting jackets. Ahead loomed a limitless expanse of flat grazing land, broken only by a nearby open pothole, glittering in the midday sun. But if our eyes stung with sweat, our mouths also watered in anticipation, for in that pothole, in plain view, hundreds of ducks were diving for their dinners. Mat sucked in his breath as he lifted his head for a wary look.

"Glory be," he whispered. "It looks like all the ducks in the world have ganged up here."

"Get down!" I snapped. "Or all the ducks in the world will take off for parts unknown."

Silently, Mat and I continued to gaze at the marvel. Never in our years of hunting together all over North America had we seen ducks in such vast numbers or curious variety. We could pick out a few teal in the bunch, but most of the others were strangers, birds with curiously shaped bills and unusual markings. But regardless of their beaks or plumage, they were sure enough wild ducks. They stood up on their hind ends to stretch and flap their wings, preened their breasts and wiggled their tail feathers, chattering cheerfully to one another just like their Yankee cousins. This, to a pair of game-starved shooters, promised good gunning and still better eating. We pulled down our heads and crawled nearer.

We worked forward until we could see the gold coloration in some of their eyes. Even if they flushed wild we'd still get a couple of shots. We slipped off our safeties and sat on our heels. The ducks ignored us. We scrambled to our feet, guns ready—and those dumb Argentine ducks still went on about their affairs. Mat slipped his gun under his arm and clapped his hands. They didn't stir. We yelled and whistled, waving our guns to make them fly. No action. Mat wiped the sweat from his eyebrows and shook his head.

"Beats anything I ever saw," he grunted. "Argentine ducks must be deaf and dumb."

"Let's rush 'em," I proposed, and we lumbered forward, yelling and waving our arms. The ducks didn't even look up.

"Let's give 'em a broadside."

At the water's edge, with a shoal of ducks almost underfoot, Mat raised his 12 and let go a single barrel right over their heads. The ducks eyed him curiously and went back to their dapping. Mat wiped his brow with his hat and pawed his sweaty hair. "Well, I'll be—" he snorted.

Then a familiar voice broke in behind us. "My Yankee friends," it was saying in an Oxford accent tinged with a trace of Spanish, "as I have warned you, it is not possible to shoot the Argentine ducks in the North American way, no more than you can shoot the North American ducks in the Argentine way."

We turned to face Guillermo Leloir, whose family owned the estancia, or ranch, where Mat and I had been invited to shoot. Beside him, a broad smile on his round face, stood Jorge Luro, Señor Leloir's friend and the pilot who had just flown us in from Buenos Aires. Both men wore I-told-you-so smiles. This was back in the prewar days, and they had been helping me in my negotiations with the Argentine government concerning a flock of scout bombers. Señor Leloir had given me some sage counsel. Now he gave me some more.

"We Latins," he said, "admire the initiative and enterprise of you North Americans, but as for your duck hunting—" He shrugged his expressive shoulders and walked away.

I glared at Mat as though it were all his fault. An old schoolmate, he was connected with the American Embassy at B.A. Dropping in on him one morning, I'd caught him sitting behind his desk with his duck gun in one hand and a trip string in the other, practicing his swing on a miniature duck as it soared across the room. Of course, that setup could lead but to one thing, the present duck shoot and the accompanying warning from Señor Leloir.

"No one shoots the ducks in Argentina," he had assured us. "So the pampas near one of our estancias fairly swarms with them. There you find many little lakes and ponds, each with vast numbers of birds on it. But, my friends," he concluded, "these you cannot shoot in the North American way."

Of course we two experienced wildfowlers had ignored the warning. That's why we were standing there in the hot sun, complete with hip boots, heavy canvas coats, pants and the other paraphernalia of the northern gunner. And our friends had the laugh on us.

Guillermo Leloir was a dapper young Argentine, dark and distin-guished in the native gaucho costume he affected on his estancia. His smartly tailored, single-breasted jacket buttoned down the front, and his full-cut trousers were tucked into the tops of short leather boots, not with the careless abandon of a North American cowboy but with the smart dash of a boulevardier. A flat-topped, stiff-brimmed black gaucho hat sat jauntily on his head, secured by a loose thong tied under his chin. In this distinctive costume our young friend looked to be exactly what he was, an Argentine aristocrat.

Jorge Luro was a big, round-faced fellow in a loose business suit and a beret. One of Argentina's pioneer sportsman-pilots, he had been the first to fly over the treacherous Andes Mountains. He had also raced automobiles in such classics as the Milan Grand Prix. Now, as he measured us in our strange regalia, he too smiled and shrugged his eloquent shoulders. Luro spoke no English, but he didn't need to with shoulders like those.

Señor Leloir, waving toward the grove of Lombardy poplars bordering the formal gardens at the ranch house, suggested we return there for lunch. "After the lunch," he said, "we will take our siesta, in the Argentine way, and then we will hunt the ducks—also in the Argentine way."

Lunch was an adventure in itself. We four sat around a long, carved, antique table in a room adorned with hunting trophies and Indian curios. Course after course was served us. When, after a while, half a broiled chicken was placed before me, I naturally supposed the main course had arrived. However, this turned out to be just another appetizer, topping off the asado for which Argentina is famous. For this they spread-eagle a dressed sheep on a long spit driven slantwise into the ground and barbecue it before a hot fire.

Even after that it was a long time before we finally came to the main dish—thick fillets of Argentine beef. During dinner Señor Leloir entertained us with vivid tales of the Argentine pampas, a subject as romantic to him as our West is to us.

"Our gaucho," he remarked, pushing back his chair, "is like your cowboy—a wild, romantic fellow. You see, I've seen a great many of your movies. But unlike your cowboy, who appears to be a devil-may-care sort, our gaucho has long been a melancholy wanderer, often a fugitive from the military press gang or the sheriff. So he took to the wide-open spaces.

"A gaucho despises firearms," he said. "His knife and his bolas are to him both weapons and implements of chase." Stepping to the wall behind him, he lifted off an old bolas. It consisted of three round stones, each covered with woven rawhide shrunk tight, and each suspended separately from the common center by a short length of braided rawhide. Holding the bolas by its center, our host swung the balls in an arc overhead.

"In pursuit of an ostrich, for example," he continued, "the gaucho rides at full speed behind the fleeing bird, twirling the bolas before he throws. The bolas, if well aimed, sails through the air and wraps around the legs of the bird, bringing it to earth. And it makes a wicked instrument with which to club a man to death."

"What," Mat inquired, "does the gaucho live on?"

"Meat and maté," Leloir replied. "Meat such as you have just eaten, prepared in the form of the asado, and yerba maté such as you may now sample."

A waiter had brought in a silver tray and set it in front of Señor Leloir. On it a silver teapot steamed over a spirit lamp, and a polished gourd, open at the top and decorated with heavy silver mountings, sat upright in a stand formed of silver leaves opening upward.

"Maté," Señor Leloir instructed, pointing to the gourd. A long silver tube, something like a soda straw with strainer holes in its lower end, stood upright in the gourd. That was a bombilla, Leloir explained. Then he spooned what looked like tea leaves into the gourd. "Yerba," he explained. "A bitter evergreen tea. Sometimes it is sold in your country as Paraguay tea."

Our host slowly filled the gourd with steaming water from the silver kettle and let the brew steep awhile. Then he took a sip of the liquid through the bombilla and passed it to me. Sure enough, it tasted just like the Paraguay tea mother used to push on us kids with the sulfur and molasses.

Leloir stepped to a glass-fronted cabinet at the end of the room. He drew out an English shotgun and passed it around to be admired.

"Relatively few Argentines are bird shooters," he remarked. "My father, who was educated in France, passed the sport on to me. I enjoyed the Scottish shooting while I studied at Oxford, and I've shot quail in Carolina, grouse and woodcock in New England and New Brunswick. . . . "

Mat's eyes began to sparkle. "What, no ducks ?" he demanded.

Leloir grinned. "In Argentina, no," he replied. "In America, yes. I hunted at Currituck in North Carolina, in Illinois, and especially for the mallard at Stuttgart, Arkansas."

"Why not here in Argentina?" Mat insisted.

"In Argentina," Leloir replied, "I prefer other sports. For example the perdiz, our South American quail, affords good shooting, though he is a runner and does not lie well like your bobwhite. But I am really more of a fisherman. Fishing for the dorada on the River Paraná is something which only your tarpon fishing can approach."

Leloir rose and moved toward the door. "Let us now take our siesta," he said. "After that we will have our duck shoot."

We were aroused from our nap by the roar of an engine exhaust under our window. It was Luro in an ancient 12-cylinder touring car with a right-hand drive. The top had been removed. Luro raced the motor with its cutout open, and the roar brought Señor Leloir from his room with two beautiful Purdey guns in his arms. Mat and I wasted no time getting downstairs.

Mat sat in the front seat with Luro; I shared the rear one with Leloir. At my feet lay an open case of American shotgun shells. Then Luro raced the motor, Leloir barked a command and we careened down the dirt road and through a gate. Swinging on two wheels, we roared out onto the open pampas, headed straight for the very pothole where Mat and I had met our Waterloo.

Driving like a wild Indian, Luro bore down on the big flock at the water's edge. And he didn't stop! The car leaped into the shallows and veered to the right, splashing a sheet of spray over the surprised wildfowl. Luro raced the motor with a terrifying roar. A shoal of squawking, protesting birds sprang into the air. Instantly we three gunners staggered to our feet, struggling to keep our balance in the pitching car, and blasted them with both barrels. Out of the tail of my eye I could see birds splashing into the water. A few quail, scared up from the grass, mingled with the fluttering ducks.

But our driver paused not for the fallen. Instead he tore off across the pampas, headed for another pothole. As the jolting car spilled me onto the rear seat, a corral gate opened and two gauchos rode hell-for-leather toward us. Splashing into the water at full speed, they yanked back on their reins, bringing their horses up with forelegs pawing the air. The gauchos, leaning from their saddles, snatched up the dead birds on long looped wires. Then they galloped after us in full cry. Mat's eyes bulged.

"Good night," he yelled. "Galloping gaucho gillies!"

Meanwhile the old car, hitting only the high spots, bounced across the pampas toward the next pothole. This time our pilot started his turn a little too late, throwing a deluge of water into the car. Wiping my eyes so I could see for a shot, I caught a glimpse of Mat standing straddle-legged on the front seat, firing with grim determination while rivulets ran down from his hat. Leloir swayed beside me, grinning, as Mat, the old warhorse, let out a whoop that brought wild yelps from all four of us. Firing and yelling, we splashed more ducks into that lagoon, where the hard-riding gauchos swept them into their bags.

This was no easy shooting. In the lurching car it was hard enough to keep your feet, let alone swing and shoot. No sooner would we abandon one pothole than we'd be off across country for the next one, still yelling like Comanches. And judging by my own snap-shooting, I began to have a sneaking suspicion that Leloir was accounting for more than his share of birds.

On one run between potholes we flushed an enormous hare, far bigger than our Western jackrabbits and as swift as chain lightning. Our driver, watching the fast-jumping rabbit out of the corner of one eye, held the car behind him while we blasted with all we had. Then, after we'd closed the range a bit, Leloir, who had not been shooting at the rabbit, sent him rolling head over heels with one shot. Leaving him to the mercy of our galloping gillies, we sped on to the next pond.

A short distance beyond this one, while we were trying to regain our balance in the car, Luro slammed the brakes on so hard I thought Mat would do a swan dive over the hood. Our pilot had sighted a perdiz speeding along a cow path. As the car ground to a squealing stop, we leaped out and took off after the running bird. But he managed to keep just ahead of us, refusing to fly. Putting on a burst of speed that brought him into the air, I stubbed my toe on a hummock and sprawled flat on my face. Leloir dropped the bird with stylish grace.

Getting under way once more, we sought out bigger, better potholes, cruising the circumference of a wide semicircle with the tall poplars of the estancia as its center. This permitted the hard-pressed gauchos to cut cross-country and keep pace with us. Thus we sped from pothole to pothole, firing as fast as we could load, taking anything and everything that came our way, on the ground or in the air. After a while we lost sight of our gauchos.

By the time we completed a half-circle around the estancia, I was ready to call it a day, though Mat would probably have kept it up until dark. My shoulder ached from the recoil of one of Mat's guns, which was too short for me; and the second finger of my trigger hand had a lump on it as big as a robin's egg where the trigger guard had bashed me. I was dripping sweat and my boots were half full of water.

Back at the estancia we spread our mixed bag on the lawn; and it was well mixed. Leloir sorted out the ducks and named some for us. Aside from the teal, which he said had probably migrated all the way from North America, these were purely local types. For instance, there were ducks with red bills and green feathers along the leading edges of their wings. Others were brown all over with dark bills. Among the quail, the perdiz chica was somewhat larger than our bobwhite and certainly a lot leggier. One variety of quail wore a topknot. The perdiz colorado, as large as a small hen turkey, was a mottled reddish-brown. Altogether we had collected over 50 birds, firing about 100 shells apiece.

Mat and I were both enthusiastic, and of course that made our host happy.

"What is your honest opinion of this hunting?" Leloir asked me.

"Well," I hedged, "I miss some things. For instance, I like to break out of a warm bed before dawn and hustle into the warmest gear I can find. I like to feel my way down to the marsh, where the punt lies on the shore, and to hear the crackle of skim ice as I pole her down the creek to the blind. Then too, it's nice to sit there behind fresh-cut cedars, shivering with excitement, fondling your old 12 as you listen to the whistle of wild wings.

"Better still, I like to watch the birds dipping and tipping up among the decoys while the dawn breaks, and to listen to their chatter as they feed among the shallows. Then, just before sunrise, I like to stand up in the blind and watch them spring out of the water, quacking and protesting. Then they straighten out and you drop a nice double. Best of all, I like to watch my old springer as he jumps into the icy water to retrieve the duck. And when, finally, he lays the birds down at my feet and looks up for a word of approval, I quit shivering and glow all over, happy just to be out there."

I stopped for breath. Leloir was translating it for Jorge Luro. When he finished, both of them smiled.

"And besides," I went on, all warmed now, "between the retrieving of a good springer and a hard-riding gaucho, I go for the dog every time."

Señor Leloir slapped his leg and laughed. "That's it!" he cried. "Just what I was telling you. That's the North American way. There's nothing I like better myself—when I'm up north."

I grinned. "And if I can't get the home-grown product," I said, "I'll take the Argentine way anytime!"

BULLHEADED - A bullhead minnow that apparently swam into the hole of a discarded pop-top can in Lake Ina was safe from bigger fish but got so much washed-in food through the opening that it grew too big to escape. The "canned" fish was discovered by Mrs. Alma Valander of Minneapolis when she picked up the can by chance. Hearing something inside after emptying the water, she opened the can and out popped the bullhead to swim off toward an uncertain fate.
- Gerry Rafferty, FARGO (ND) FORUM.

BUMPER CROP - When George Green of Barrington, New Hampshire, got home late with a dent in the front end of his car, he didn't get anywhere with his story of a buck deer running into him until he persuaded his wife to go out with him to the scene. As they approached the place, a second buck bounded out of the woods and smacked into the radiator grill.
- WM. H. Ridings, LAWRENCE (MA) EAGLE.

CLOSE SHAVE - Peering at his beard he had pledged to let grow until he killed his first deer, F. H. Allen of Houston saw something moving in the mirror and whirled in time to drop a buck that had sneaked into camp.
- Bob Brister, HOUSTON (TX) CHRONICLE.